Shipbreaker Extraordinaire
Harry Pounds of Portsmouth

Richard Holme

Dedicated to my lovely grandchildren,
Toby and Fliss.

First published in Great Britain in 2026 by
Seaforth Publishing
An imprint of
Pen & Sword Books Ltd
Yorkshire – Philadelphia

ISBN 978 1 0361 3360 3 (HARDBACK)
ISBN 978 1 0361 3362 7 (EPUB)

The Publisher's authorised representative in the EU for product safety is Authorised Rep
Compliance Ltd., Ground Floor, 71 Lower Baggot Street, Dublin D02 P593, Ireland.
www.arccompliance.com

Designed and typeset by Ian Hughes, Mousemat Design Limited
Printed and bound in India by Replika Press Pvt Ltd

CONTENTS

ABBREVIATIONS

ASP	Admiralty Salvage Pontoon
grt	Gross Registered Tonnage
HDML	Harbour Defence Motor Launch
LARC	Lighter, Amphibious, Resupply, Cargo
LCF	Landing Craft Flak
LCI	Landing Craft Infantry
LCM	Landing Craft Mechanised
LCT	Landing Craft Tank
LST	Landing Ship Tank
ML	Motor Launch
MMS	Motor Minesweeper
MOD	Ministry of Defence
MTB	Motor Torpedo Boat
NMM	National Maritime Museum
NMRN	National Museum of the Royal Navy
NSC	Naval Servicing Craft
'Old Harry'	Henry George Pounds (1897–1971)
RMAS	Royal Maritime Auxiliary Service
The News	*Portsmouth News* (newspaper)
TNA	The National Archives
VHF	Van Heyghen Frères (Ghent shipbreakers)
WO	War Office
WSS	World Ship Society
'Young Harry'	Henry Frederick Pounds (1924–96)

CHAPTER 1

INTRODUCTION: A UNIQUE FAMILY BUSINESS

After around 150 years in operation, the Pounds business closed in 2023. Previously, thousands of visitors to Portsmouth have driven past the Pounds yard each year, the vast majority oblivious to its extraordinary history. Much of the UK's military heritage has passed through Pounds, including hundreds of historic ships and military vehicles, and even aircraft and locomotives at times. Although a large quantity of this has been cut up for scrap, the majority has been resold for further use or indeed, on occasions, earmarked for long-term preservation.

There are plans afoot to develop Pounds' former Tipner base in Portsmouth. I have been fortunate enough to be able to gather information about the business from the current Harry Pounds, his brother John and the late Tony Pounds-Cornish. Several visits to their fascinating yard since 1991 have been extremely helpful. More recently I have been kindly lent the extant records of the business – some dating back to 1935 – as well as the Pounds photographic collection. I owe a substantial debt also to many maritime historians, including Philip Simons, Dr Ian Buxton, Stephen Wenham, Dave Sowdon, David Asprey and David Fricker.

The focus of this book is on ships, but in two chapters the purchases of military vehicles and aircraft have been covered. Nearly 600 ships and boats were bought by Pounds and a detailed schedule of all these with a commentary is included in Appendix 2.

Every effort has been made to obtain copyright permission on all images. Pictures are by the author unless otherwise stated. Many are undated, and a few, while conveying the atmosphere of the yard, are not of the very best quality.

Richard Holme, Saltwood, July 2025

CHAPTER 2

ORIGINS

Portsmouth Dockyard was one of the largest industrial complexes in southern England during the nineteenth century. Besides its own labour force of several thousand, its existence and needs spawned many smaller ancillary businesses locally – including Pounds. Frederick Pounds had founded the Pounds business by 1875.[1]

He was born in 1837 at Wimborne, Dorset, and like many at the time, probably initially moved to Portsmouth to work in the busy naval dockyard. Frederick's business is described variously as a 'general dealer' and 'wardrobe dealer' operating from Crasswell Street, Portsmouth, not too far from the Dockyard gates.[2]

Frederick married Elizabeth Baker in Portsmouth in June 1867. She originated from the remote Devon village of Luppitt, a hard-working farming community in the harsh environment of the Blackdown Hills.[3] Perhaps to better herself she then moved to Dorset, where she met Frederick and they moved to Portsmouth together.[4] There were others by the name of Pounds already in Portsmouth, including a Henry George Pounds in Dean Street, but these, contrary to some accounts, were not apparently connected to Frederick's business. Portsmouth benefactor John Pounds (1776–1839), the renowned founder of free common schools, was Frederick's great uncle but not involved at all in the business.[5]

The surname Pounds originated, according to tradition, from the family's involvement long ago in the rustling of cattle from pounds – enclosures in which in years gone by, stray animals would have been held. It is understood also that many elements of the family were historically involved in smuggling.

Many wooden sailing ships were being broken up in Portsmouth at the time Pounds' business was getting under way, and it is clear from contemporary accounts that this was a lucrative business. The main value would be in the copper fastenings and sheathing (if any). Hardwood in the hull could be recycled for making furniture or flooring, but softwood might often be burnt or possibly sold as firewood or fencing. The shipbreaking activity seems to have been concentrated in the Camber as well as at Pesthouse Field, now part of the Dockyard. The entrepreneurs involved in this industry would have used convict labour in part. In addition to the uses noted above, much of the wood and fittings would be recycled in the Dockyard for use as jetties, slipways, storehouses and so on,[6] while some would be auctioned off, in all probability to businesses like Pounds.

In 1883 Elizabeth Pounds took over the business following the death of her husband Frederick. By then it was described as a 'marine store dealer', so already quite probably trading in surplus material from the Dockyard.

Elizabeth died in 1889 and her son, another Frederick Pounds, took over the business at the age of just 20. He moved the operation to nearby Voller Street in 1901. Trading in wood still seems to have been part of the business, involving no doubt the recycling of timber from sailing ships broken up locally by others. The business moved to 2 Common Street in Landport, Portsmouth, around 1909.[7]

After the First World War, the Royal Navy had a huge surplus of redundant shipping, worn out from war service, no longer needed or simply not affordable in peace time. Many new shipbreaking operations sprang up around the country to deal with this new source of metal. Pounds was one of these and in 1921 purchased for the first time a number of ships for demolition. Both British and German submarines were acquired, as well as other small yard vessels that were surplus to naval requirements. They were broken up at Quay Street in Fareham, near Portsmouth, and possibly also in the Camber in Portsmouth itself. Demolition work may have been subcontracted to third parties.

By the 1920s, Frederick Pounds was described as a 'metal merchant' at 38–9 Arundel Street, Landport, Portsmouth. By 1921 he had also built and opened the Trafalgar Cinema in Portsmouth and subsequently operated it until at least 1927. Torpedo tubes formed the entrance pillars. Family legend suggests that a large consignment of surplus army boots, all left-footed, was deployed as part of the foundations. His son, Harry Pounds (born 1897) was trading at St John's Road in Fratton, Portsmouth, as a 'general dealer'. His notepaper (pictured on the next page) demonstrates the very wide range of services offered by his business. Father and son worked closely together.

Harry had served in the 4th Hampshire Regiment in the First World War and then flew DH.9s in the Royal Flying Corps, being commissioned as a Second Lieutenant in March 1919.[8] Initially regarded as something of a playboy after the war, he was to throw himself into the business from 1923 and over the years, put a tremendous amount of energy and skill into its development.

Submarine *D8* was bought by Pounds for demolition in 1921. *(NMRN)*

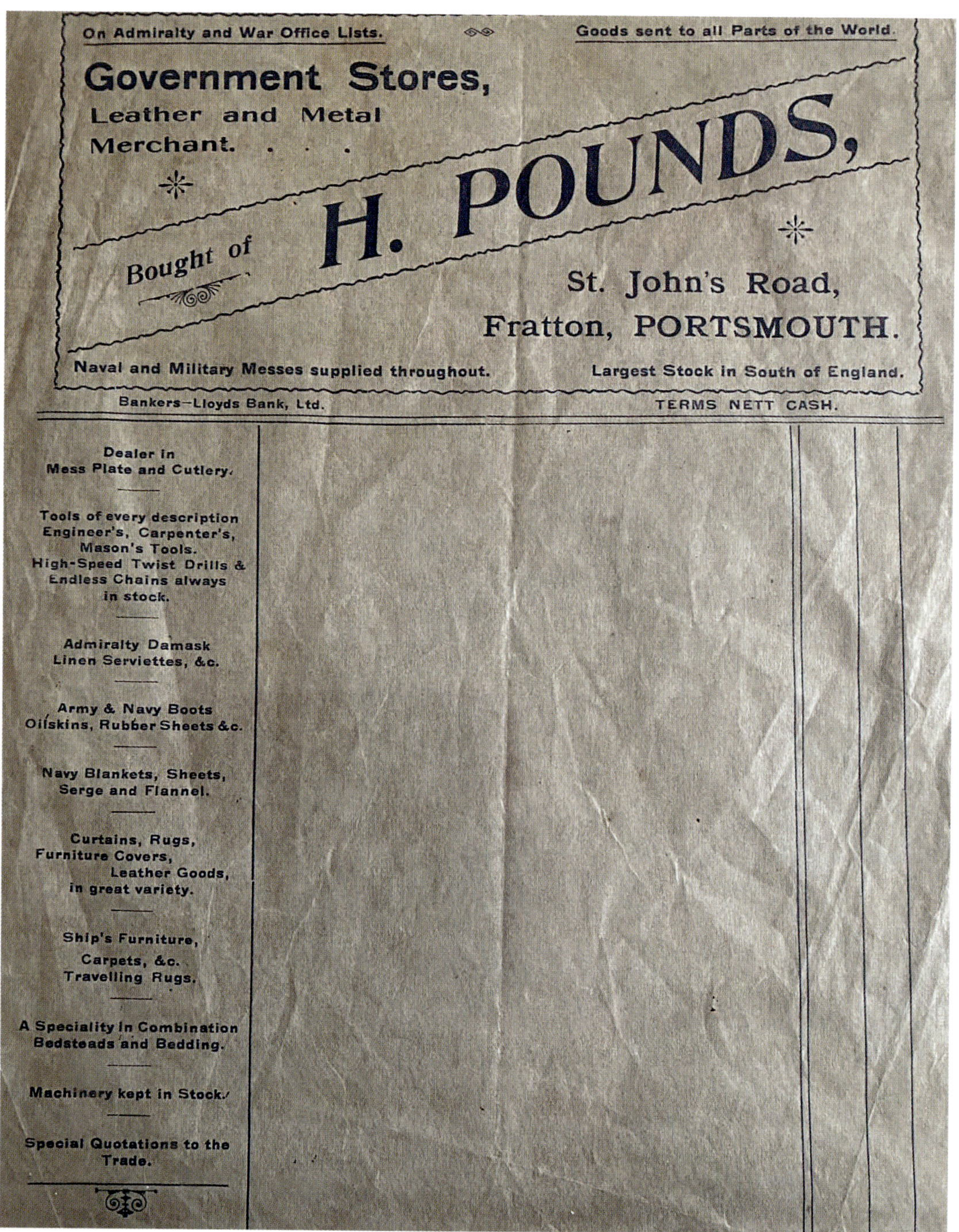

Besides ship dismantling, the Pounds businesses also dealt in land scrap and military surplus, such as uniforms and boots. In addition, there was general demolition work such as the dismantling in 1921 of St Mary's Colewort Church, Portsmouth. The Pounds family also started to acquire property in Old Portsmouth, a shrewd investment as in time that area became fashionable, and property prices took off.

Above: Frederick Pounds
(1869–1939). *(Pounds)*

Prior to the acquisition of a base at Portchester, Pounds broke up some wrecks in Fountain Lake by Whale Island in Portsmouth harbour. The first was the former gunboat *Insolent*, which was had been serving as a gate vessel when wrecked in Fountain Lake.

The German torpedo boat destroyers *V44* and *V82* were an unusual acquisition in 1927. *V44* had served at Jutland and both units had surrendered on cessation of hostilities in 1918. After they and other units of the High Seas Fleet had attempted to scuttle themselves at Scapa Flow in June 1919, a Royal Navy boarding party intervened to beach smaller units, including *V44* and *V82*, on the island of Fara in the Orkneys.

Salvaged and then taken to Portsmouth, they were used for target practice from October to December 1920, being battered by the monitor HMS *Terror*. After being beached, they were sold to large shipbreakers T.W. Ward in March 1921, who in turn sold them on to Pounds. They were stripped by Pounds as they lay beached on mud flats by Fountain Lake in Portsmouth harbour. It is clear, though, that Pounds did not fully demolish the hulks as their cut-down hulls were still visible when examined by the Maritime Archaeology Trust in 2015.[9] One curiosity is that in 1964 Pounds made a number of payments in connection with scrap gear from *V44* possibly sold on to 'Metal and Ropes'.[10] Maybe further scrap was extracted at that time or work was done to prevent the *V44* wreck being an obstruction in the busy Portsmouth harbour.

V82 in Fountain Lake, Portsmouth, c. 1920 – painting by William Wylie.
(© National Maritime Museum, Greenwich, London).

CHAPTER 3

TRAFALGAR WHARF, PORTCHESTER: A FIRST BASE

Acquisition and Expansion of the Yard

In November 1924 Frederick and Harry Pounds acquired land at Portchester on the northern reaches of Portsmouth harbour.[11] This was the first permanent base for the expanding business, becoming known as Trafalgar Wharf. Pounds were to operate there until 1968.

Family tradition has it that this land was won in a game of cards. They then successfully sought permission to reclaim some of the adjacent foreshore and build a wharf and pier. This land had initially been reclaimed by French and Dutch prisoners of war in Napoleonic times,[12] and by the 1920s was still farmland – the Portchester Farm Estate. Parts were also being developed for residential use. Pounds were, however, quite open in disclosing their intentions to open a scrap and shipbreaking yard there.

It was unsurprising that concern was expressed by those who had bought building plots on 'greenfield' land adjacent to the Pounds site:

… owners are seriously alarmed at the proposal to sanction the erection of jetties etc by Mr Pounds. The area is one that is eminently suitable for residential purposes, and it is the wish and hope of every owner in the neighbourhood that it may remain so and that the neighbourhood may be protected from industrial and commercial encroachments.[13]

It seems curious therefore that the Pounds business was allowed to operate in this quiet residential area. Why was this? The Admiralty had no objection but equally they had no local knowledge or concerns. It helped that Pounds readily made concessions to get the necessary permissions, agreeing to remove existing temporary buildings and that there would be no smoke or unsightly buildings. A proposed timber pond would not be built. It was recognised by the authorities that sometimes industrial buildings would, through necessity, need to be sited close to a residential area. After all, most of the Pounds business would be based on reclaimed land, below the high-water mark.

Harry Pounds (1897–1971) – 'Old Harry'. *(Pounds)*

Two letterheads from the 1920s.

In the end it seems all were content with the concept of the scrapyard being based on the foreshore at Portchester, except for some aggrieved residents.

Although Frederick Pounds helped to instigate the Portchester operation, correspondence indicates that it was his son Harry who was running the business at the time. Harry's impressive headed notepaper (above) recites the broad nature of his activities.

Frederick Pounds tended to correspond on notepaper from the Trafalgar Cinema, which was one of his other businesses (as previously mentioned).

The main trade at this time was very much dealing in scrap and equipment, shipbreaking being only a minor element. There was also shingle dealing, conducted by father and son together, as indicated by trade directories and the notepaper above. This business may well have had its own dredger for this purpose.

After gaining permission for a new wharf and jetty in April 1927, Frederick Pounds acquired the underlying land for £100. However, a dispute ensued when Pounds built a further wharf without permission. Retrospective approval for this was eventually granted in 1929 and the underlying land sold to them for £95. Pounds then wished to extend the wharf by 100ft. The Board of Trade refused permission, requesting first that improvements be made to the way the business operated. Harry Pounds was somewhat indignant at these objections; he was merely looking to possess the land needed to accommodate his expanding business. The letter below demonstrates his attitude.

Mercantile Marine Dept
Board of Trade   *10th March 1926*

Gentlemen
Re yours of the 3rd inst regarding the reclaiming of certain foreshore below high watermark at Portchester, the constructed jetty when finished will be mostly used for the dismantling of H.M. ships and boats, also to land sand and shingle. There will be no obnoxious trade or works, smoke stacks erected on the site. I might add that since writing last to you, I have purchased the remaining plot of land which now forms the whole of the western side of the Portchester Road, from Messrs Hall Pain and Foster who on behalf of Mr Cooper are now applying to you for a removal of mud with which to make cement.

I feel convinced that any previous objections which these people made (if any) must be withdrawn owing to the nature of their application.

I should like to add in passing that we have quite a considerable number of men who at the moment are only being employed in a very obsolete manner,

owing to the fact we have no available wharf to carry on our work. I should be very obliged if you would give this matter your earliest consideration as I do not wish to discharge any more of my men who have been long and trusted servants.
Yours respectfully

H.G. Pounds.[14]

The Board of Trade were involved as they were responsible for protecting and administering the foreshore, which was owned by the Crown.

Land was quite legitimately reclaimed by Pounds through the dumping of materials which included brick rubble, plaster, paper, ceiling laths, broken slates, roofing felt and scrap iron.[15] Locals complained this was a breeding ground for rats and that debris would float away on the high tide. However, investigations by the Medical Officer of Health for Portsmouth could find no dangers whatsoever to public health.[16] There were also practical concerns about maintenance of the sea wall and in allowing drainage from the surrounding houses. Pounds, though, were just continuing the process of land reclamation that had begun in Napoleonic times. Even the elderly Frederick Pounds would turn his hand to this 'shovelling' to help the efforts of the reclamation gang.

Harry's nephew, Tony Pounds-Cornish (1930–2022) recalls gang members such as 'Black Pete' (renowned for his black moustache) and 'Scabby Way' fighting during hard-earned lunch breaks. Tony began work as an 8-year-old, delivering water to the labour force in hot weather. He was to become a vital member of the business in future years, managing the yard.

A Huge and Unusual Acquisition – HMS *Donegal*

One of the ships bought by Pounds almost escaped complete demolition – the former first-rate wooden screw battleship *Donegal*, built in 1858. She had been undertaking a useful retirement as HMS *Vernon*, part of the Royal Navy torpedo training school in Portsmouth harbour. This had been located at Portchester Creek since 1895 but in 1923 it was decided to bring the school onshore at the Gunwharf in Portsmouth. *Donegal* therefore became redundant and was sold off to Pounds in 1925 for £3,707. However, she sank while under tow and had to be scrapped in situ offshore – a challenging task. Her wreck became infested with conger eels. The structure contained valuable 9ft copper rods which had to be hammered out; there was consternation when copper bolts sprang out and were lost in the mud. Non-ferrous metals such as copper are particularly valuable to any shipbreaker.

However, a shipbreaker may find timber harder to sell and, in some cases, it sadly ends up being burned. It is known, though, that teak from *Donegal* was sold in 1926 for use in the building of the Old Ship Inn at Brighouse in Yorkshire. In June 2023, the author visited the pub and photographed some of these timbers, as well as elaborate carved wood from the frontage that may well have graced the stern of *Donegal*, but equally could have been the work of a local craftsman in Brighouse in the 1920s.

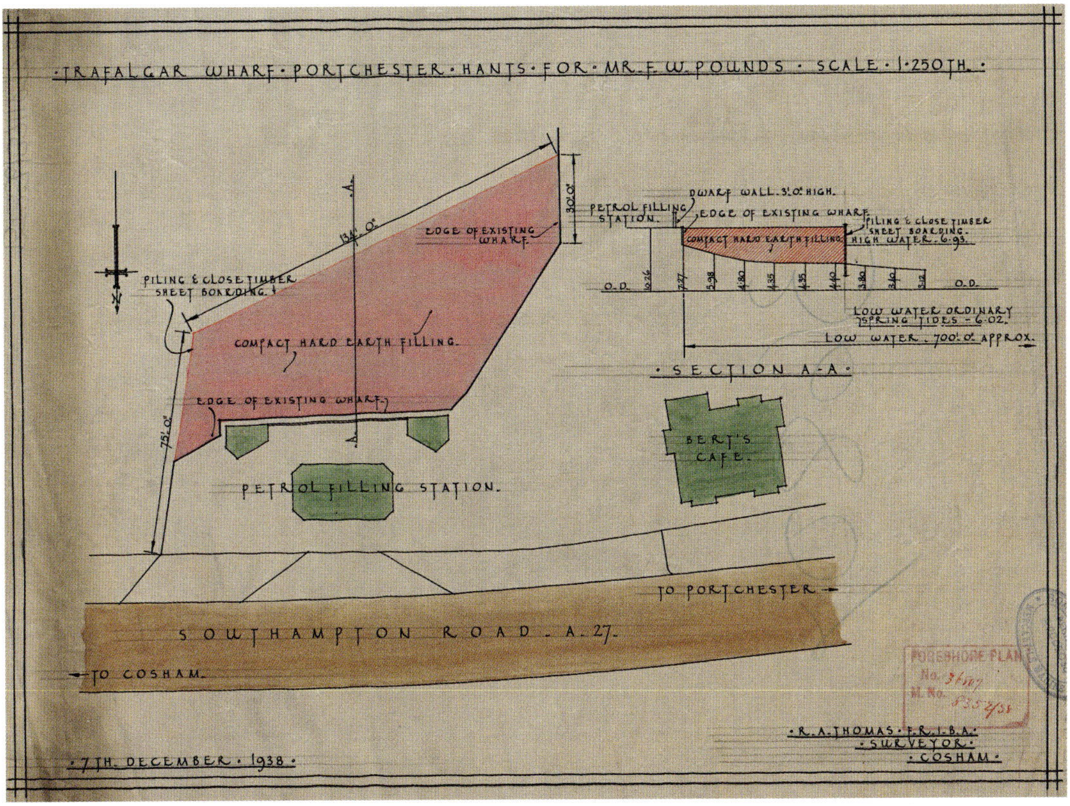

Plans dating from 1938 for further extension of the Portchester yard through foreshore reclamation.
Note how the yard was hemmed in by the A27, a petrol station and Bert's Café.
(TNA BT356/3712)

Donegal (right) when serving at HMS *Vernon* torpedo school. *(Paul Brown collection)*

The Old Ship Inn, Brighouse.

Later, in 1936/7, several tons of teak from *Donegal* were sold to the Society for Nautical Research to assist in their restoration of their wooden walls, *Implacable* and *Foudroyant*. Pounds kindly gave at least one year's credit to the Society to facilitate their charitable endeavours.[17]

Continuing complaints from neighbours focused on what became known as the 'derelicts', particularly the hulk of the *Donegal* and a 'battle float' (target), which had both arrived in 1925. They lay there for many years with little or no demolition work taking place, despite assurances from Pounds that this would occur. Sometimes the weather was blamed for the delay, sometimes the state of the tide. Pounds made references to (unspecified) High Court action with a third party concerning the derelicts, preventing their break-up. In 1936 Pounds were ordered to put lights and markings on their two derelicts as they had become a hazard to navigation. There were other derelicts, but Pounds protested that these were not their ships. Pounds were told that unless progress was made in removing the derelicts, they would not be granted permission for the jetty extension.

The *Donegal* was a very substantial wooden ship, hard to dismantle and not very profitable, once valuable items such as her copper bolts had been extracted. Demolition was tricky as 'Old Harry' Pounds commented in November 1936:

> *… here we are confronted with all manner of difficulties, and it is naturally a lengthy job to completely remove. I can however state that in spite of our adversities, work will be carried on continuously wherever possible so that the whole of the* Donegal *will be removed in the least possible time.*[18]

Indeed, in 1937, a frank note on the Board of Trade file confirms this:

> *Mr Pounds will apparently ignore everybody if he can and it seems that the only way of bringing him to heel is to send him a stiff letter from the Solicitors Department threatening immediate proceedings….*[19]

The remnants of *Donegal* can still be seen in the background in the 1955 film *The Ship that Died of Shame*, filmed in part at Pounds yard at Portchester.

Expansion of the Business

Besides *Donegal* and the German destroyers mentioned above, ships acquired by Pounds for break-up in the 1920s and 1930s were generally wrecks, small yard craft and tugs. Company records and photos confirm that the core business remained land scrap and the resale of equipment such as boilers and generators. Shipbreaking was a sideline. Some residents adjacent to Trafalgar Wharf continued to be unhappy, having their views down Portsmouth harbour spoiled by the Pounds yard. Indeed, some signed petitions in 1936 and 1939 asking for the Board of Trade to act.

In January 1939, the Admiralty even ceased trading with Pounds for a while due to the ongoing dispute with the Board of Trade on the lack of progress in clearing the derelicts.

In May 1939 Pounds sold part of their land southwest of Trafalgar Wharf to boat builders Vospers, who needed new premises after their yard at Flathouse Shipyard, Portsmouth, was compulsorily purchased by the Admiralty in 1938. Having acquired the land, Vospers started trading there in around 1940. This land now sits well inshore due to more recent land reclamation.[20] Further land was sold by Pounds to Vospers in 1942, but Pounds continued to trade at the remainder of their Trafalgar Wharf site until 1968.

The business was quieter than normal during the Second World War, with a number of staff away on military duties. There was some work in clearing and scrapping wrecks; for example, the passenger ship *Marmion*, a minesweeper in wartime, was sunk by air attack in Harwich and her remains cut up by Pounds.

The cessation of hostilities in 1945 led to many more opportunities for Pounds as an abundance of surplus naval vessels became available, as had happened after the First World War.

One interesting purchase was the former American submarine *P556* in 1947. She was in a poor condition following a battery explosion at Portsmouth, thus

P556 in wartime. A Wren team can be seen preparing to hoist a torpedo on board the submarine at HMS *Dolphin* at Gosport, Portsmouth harbour. *(NMRN)*

LCI (L) *254. (Pounds)*

Left: *DUKW* coming ashore from *Warspite*, seen in the background by St Michael's Mount, *c.* 1954. *(Author's collection)*

Below: LCT (4) *868. (Pounds)*

Pounds, being local, were obvious purchasers. She was initially moored off the Portchester yard, near the site of what is now Port Solent, and later beached there in January 1949. She was to survive at Pounds for another forty-five years. Lampooned as an eyesore by many locals, she was sometimes mistaken for a U-Boat. Built in 1922 by Bethlehem Steel's shipyard at Quincy, Massachusetts, as *S23*, she was one of the ageing vessels transferred to the Royal Navy under the Lend-Lease provisions of 1941 to assist the UK war effort.

On one occasion, thieves were spotted by Pounds, plundering the *P556* hulk as it lay offshore. There was a delay though before Pounds called the police as the thieves' efforts had unwittingly 'liberated' much useful material, saving Pounds the trouble of doing so! The thieves and their scrap were detained as soon as they came ashore.

It was only in 1965 that initial reclamation work for the new motorway – the M275 – meant the hulk had to be moved away from Portchester to Pounds' new Tipner site. A local news report described her somewhat reluctant departure.

> *Rusting framework creaked and groaning debris and seaweed shot away like shrapnel as (the) former US submarine [...] slithered away from the slurping mud. Slowly the hulk, which has lain in Portchester Creek for 21 years under constant fire from view conscious local residents, was towed up the creek into Portsmouth Harbour. Its future is still not decided. Said its owner Mr Henry Pounds 'I have not made up my mind yet whether to break it up for scrap or dump it in the sea. Its most valuable components – the batteries – were taken out years ago. If after I've taken a look and valued it, I find it is not worth breaking up, I shall sink it off St Catherine's Deep.' He said his father bought it [...] in 1947 and later gave it to him.*[21]

P556 lingered at Tipner for many years. This part of her story is covered in Chapter 5, p. 81.

In 1947, and probably earlier, many landing craft were acquired and moored offshore as one local described:

> *These craft, part of which are packed very closely together like a jigsaw puzzle [...] extend a long distance from the wharf, parallel and about 200 feet from the main Cosham Fareham Road. [...] two landing craft, badly moored some months ago came ashore. I have seen no attempt to get them off.*[22]

There were rumours that Pounds were to buy fifty more of these, then moored in Poole harbour, however it is unclear whether this went ahead. These acquisitions were probably of LCIs and LCMs, although few governmental records survive of the disposal of these vessels. However, it is understood from the then Director of Small Craft Disposals, that in September 1946 some three thousand small craft had been disposed of and another two to three thousand were for sale.[23] A vast number by any standards! This presented potential business opportunities for Pounds. A motor launch or MTB (without engines) could be bought for £500–£1,000 and a 72ft HDML for £4,000–£5,000 with diesel engines. Many surplus naval craft were laid up in Portchester Creek, although it is not always clear if Pounds owned these. Pictured on p. 17, perhaps as late as 1953, is an LCT (4) *868* at Portchester. She had been built by the Warrenpoint Shipyard in 1944 but had been sold to Vernons of Chichester in 1945, who in turn must have sold it on to Pounds. Pounds may have had many of these LCT Mark 4s; they were quickly sold off after the war and were not as sturdy as other LCTs such as the Mark 3, so were less suitable for transfer to ongoing commercial service. 869 Mark 4s were built in the war, about 62 per cent of all landing craft then built.[24]

Smaller amphibious craft were also purchased, such as DUKWs. Several of these were sold to the Wolverhampton Metal Company in the early 1950s to facilitate their demolition work on the famous battleship *Warspite*, which had been wrecked off the Cornish coast. There was also discussion regarding Pounds providing a floating crane to facilitate the removal of scrap from the great battleship, but this did not materialise.

Landing Craft Infantry Large (LCI (L)) *254* and *314* were both built at the New Jersey Shipbuilding Co. and lent to the Royal Navy from early 1943 to 10 December 1946. Having seen active service in the Mediterranean and Pacific theatres, they were sold in 1946–7 to Pounds.

Later, from the 1960s, Pounds were to acquire more landing craft from owners who had bought the vessels shortly after 1945 (see pp. 46–48), and used them for commercial purposes. Purchases were also successfully made of landing craft built after 1945.

A local landmark was the old paddle steamer *Solent*. After forty-six years' service on the Portsmouth–Isle of Wight route, she was sold to Pounds in 1948. Still garbed in her wartime grey, she provided accommodation for lorry drivers using the adjacent Bert's Café. As a funnel-less and paddle-less hulk she survived in this role well into the late 1950s, before being scrapped (see photograph on p. 20).

In all, 396 motor minesweepers were built between 1940 and 1945 in response to German use of the magnetic mine and were being disposed of in the mid-1950s. Pounds acquired at least seven of these in the mid-1950s for break-up or resale.

Some scenes from the 1955 film *The Ship that Died of Shame* were filmed at Trafalgar Wharf and footage reveals a crowded but tidy facility (possibly cleared up especially for the filming?) with towering piles of scrap. Images on pp. 22–3 and in the Chapter 5 section 'Films' (p. 91) show interesting stills of filming taking place in the yard.

By the early 1950s, larger numbers of mercantile ships were being acquired and were often resold for further service rather than being demolished. Ship trading rather than shipbreaking was by then becoming more common.

The remaining part of the Trafalgar Wharf site was disposed of by Pounds in October 1968,[25] as neighbours Vospers, having merged with Thornycroft in 1966, needed the land for further expansion of their business. Pounds had in any case been using another location at Tipner, further south in the harbour, since the 1950s. Then, in 1964, they acquired land at Tipner, partly perhaps in anticipation of Vospers making an offer for Trafalgar Wharf, although there is a suggestion that the local council put Pounds under some pressure to move out of Portchester.

The paddle steamer *Solent* during her days as a café alongside the A27 at Paulsgrove in the 1940s and 1950s. (The News)

A view of Portchester, with Vospers dock in centre and Pounds' Trafalgar Wharf to the right, *c.* 1949. (*Pounds*)

A general view of Trafalgar Wharf, 1920s. *(Pounds)*

Above and below: MMS *1685* and a sister ship at Portchester. Despite her ramshackle appearance, MMS *1685* was resold for further service in 1956.
(Pounds)

A general view of the crowded Portchester yard, sadly undated. *(Pounds)*

Right: An atmospheric view at Portchester. Possibly *YC 3* or *YC 86*, a lifting/mooring vessel, can be seen to right. Both were sold to Pounds in 1928. *(Pounds)*

Left: Portchester yard, *c.* 1954. Two sea mules (former US small tugs) are visible in the foreground, along with an elegant 47ft motor passenger launch, while at the rear is *X134*, of 1915 vintage, which was converted to a cable-laying function. The photograph is from the film *The Ship that Died of Shame. (Alamy)*

Below: The dredger *Rossall*, bought from fellow shipbreakers T.W. Ward in 1963, was resold for further commercial service in the following year. *(Pounds)*

CHAPTER 4

A Scottish Base: The Purchase of Cairnryan, 1960

Pounds acquired the military port at Cairnryan in 1960. It had been built between 1941 and 1945 at a cost approaching £4m. Situated near Stranraer in southwest Scotland, it was an emergency wartime facility to be used if long-established ports such as Southampton were put out of action by heavy bombing. Another military port was built at Faslane at the same time for a similar purpose. After the war, both ports sought a fresh role. Faslane was used for shipbreaking from 1946 to 1980 and indeed Cairnryan was used for the same undertaking between 1948 and 1950 and then for the dumping of surplus ammunition and even chemical weapons at sea.[26]

This dumping activity was set to end in 1958, and several hundred locals lost their jobs as a consequence – quite a blow in such a remote area. Having confirmed that no other government department had a use for the port, the War Office engaged land agents to market it for sale. Prior to the disposal, the War Office had bought up land which provided rail access to the port so that it could be marketed in the hope that it could still be used as a working port.[27] Tenders for sale were issued in September 1959. The port comprised 235 acres onshore, together with a deepwater jetty – the 'South Deep', 2,000ft in length – and a smaller lighterage wharf, just 375ft long. Both were equipped with cranes.

In December 1959, an offer of £200,000 from Harry Pounds (Old Harry) was accepted and his purchase of the port was made through a special-purpose vehicle, Cairnryan Port Company Ltd. To minimise stamp duty, Pounds sought to maximise the allocation of proceeds to the cranes which were duty exempt. After initially claiming as much as £150,000 was attributable to the cranes, Pounds finally settled for £85,000.

Other parties had tried to buy the port and one, F.R. Evans (Leeds) Ltd, complained strongly when their bid was rejected. They were reassured that Pounds had made the highest bid.[28] Evans commented:

> *… they knew Mr Pounds and they could not think that Mr Pounds would be able to do anything at Cairnryan which would employ much labour.*[29]

The War Office had found negotiations with Pounds were protracted and referred to the transaction as a 'most difficult sale' and highlighted 'numerous difficulties' in the disposal.[30]

Sale negotiations were indeed protracted for this and other reasons. Pounds finally took possession of the site in April 1960, but before even completing on the purchase of Cairnryan, Pounds were offering the cranes for sale to potential purchasers, as recounted by the land agent in March 1960.

> *... three representatives of a Canadian oil company arrived at the Port stating they were there on the authority of Mr Pounds; again, they had no credentials to this effect. They wished to see the cranes and asked if these could be operated. The Garrison Engineer did not wish to prejudice negotiations [...] with Mr Pounds, and the cranes were tested...*[31]

Ultimately, most of the cranes were sold by Pounds for an estimated £85,000 for further service in Agadir, Morocco, where the port facilities had been damaged by an earthquake. The huge hammerhead crane remained at Cairnryan though, as did five of the lighter cranes.

Pounds had led locals to believe they had bid for or even acquired Britain's last battleship, *Vanguard*, which was offered for sale in June 1960. Curiously, as early as November 1959, Pounds had given the impression that they had purchased *Vanguard* and that she would be broken up at Cairnryan. In the end *Vanguard* was demolished by Shipbreaking Industries at Faslane, one of the two largest shipbreakers at that time. She arrived at Faslane for cutting-up in August 1960.

The South Deep Jetty at Cairnryan, replete with cranes when Pounds acquired the port in 1960. *(Pounds)*

Judging by the press report pictured on p. 27, Pounds bid £400,000 for *Vanguard*, rather less than the ultimate price accepted by the Admiralty of £540,000.

In October 1960, the Minister of Transport met with Harry Pounds to discuss the use of the port and reported:

In general, we got the impression that he is genuine in his endeavours to get the port going again but he has had no experience in these affairs and finds himself slightly frustrated on such matters as Customs facilities etc.

There was clearly a need to keep Pounds happy as, while commenting on a hotly disputed matter, the Ministry representative commented:

it is desirable that we should establish good relations with Mr Pounds…[32]

In early 1961, the port remained inactive and in consequence there was considerable disquiet locally that Pounds had not employed much, if any, of the local workforce in this economically depressed area. They had previously indicated to the War Office that they might employ around 300. Stranraer Town Council were active in pursuing this, especially when in January 1961 it was rumoured that Pounds were selling the port on. Questions were asked in Parliament by the local MP, John Brewis, about how the sale to Pounds had been permitted in the first place. After all Pounds was a small operation, employing only six people in Portsmouth.

Mr Brewis asked: 'what consultations his Department had with the British Iron and Steel Corporation before deciding that Mr HG Pounds was the most suitable purchaser to start a shipbreaking industry at Cairnryan…?'
Mr Ramsden: 'None sir'
Mr Brewis: 'Would not my hon Friend agree that the British Iron and Steel Corporation virtually controls that great industry? Is he aware that if he had consulted the Corporation it would have told him that this person was most unlikely to establish a successful shipbreaking venture at Cairnryan Port and had in fact not done so?'
Mr Ramsden: 'The sale was not conditional on the purchaser using the port for shipbreaking or in any particular way. Quite apart from the difficulties such a condition could have added to selling the property at all, I am advised that it could not have been effectively enforced in law.'[33]

Pounds had not only made the highest bid but made assurances about employing hundreds of locals. The purchase of Cairnryan was the brainchild of 'Old Harry' Pounds (1897–1971), but his son 'Young Harry' was less keen. Visits to Cairnryan by either father or son were rare. Old Harry's manager, Commander Rayner, was more frequently seen. Cairnryan is a long way from Portsmouth, over 450 miles, making communication at that time difficult.

The smaller lighterage wharf at Cairnryan was in poor condition when Pounds acquired the port in 1960. Nevertheless in 1964 Pounds managed to sell

The South Deep Jetty at Cairnryan, *c.* 1968. Note that by this date, most of the cranes had gone. The dredger *Myles Kennedy*, once owned by Pounds, can be seen to the left, being converted to a crane barge for salvage work on the HMS *Drake* wreck. *(Shipbreaking (Queenborough) Ltd photo).*

2 June 1960. *(Glasgow Herald)*

The carrier HMS *Ark Royal* approaching Cairnryan for breakup in November 1980. *(Author's collection)*

the wharf to ferry operators Atlantic Steam Navigation Company Ltd (ASN) for £25,000, to facilitate their services to Northern Ireland. The ASN company history recounts:

> *In the early Sixties, ASN began secret negotiations with Mr Pounds to acquire part of his Loch Ryan empire. These culminated when the ASN Board, albeit with some well concealed misgivings, showed great foresight in purchasing*

ten acres, known as the Lighterage Wharf. Mr Pounds was well satisfied with his sale of a near-derelict wharf to a shipping line who were ready to pay £25,000 for waterside land in a remote area of South West Scotland.

It is believed that ASN also paid £15,000 annually to Pounds in return for not allowing their larger South Deep Jetty to be used for ferry services.

A railway had been constructed between 1941 and 1945 to connect Cairnryan to the mainline at Stranraer. Trains continued to run to Stranraer for a few years following Pounds' acquisition. However, Pounds then engaged contractors to lift the railway track back to Stranraer for scrap. This took just five weeks and yielded perhaps 3,500 tons of valuable high-tensile steel. It has been estimated that Pounds and the contractors made a profit of £150,000 on lifting the railway track alone at Cairnryan, much of which would have been usefully repurposed (such as railway sleepers, some rail sections and panels), rather than recycled.[34]

Then, in May 1969, Pounds sold the port for approximately £55,000 to the Loch Ryan Harbour Company Ltd, a business owned by an Italian, Pompeio Gandini. Previously, Gandini's company had been the contractors who lifted the railway track. Gandini's Shipbreaking (Queenborough) Ltd would subsequently use the South Deep for shipbreaking until 1991. Famous ships such as the huge aircraft carriers *Eagle* and *Ark Royal* were demolished there.

The later use of Cairnryan as a leading shipbreaking centre suggests that Pounds were adept in identifying the port as potentially highly suitable for this purpose.

In June 1961, John Profumo, then War Minister, had reflected on the sale to Pounds:

I do feel badly about the way things have turned out and I should be only too happy to help in any way I could; but I'm sure you will see that our position as vendors does not really offer us any scope. The property has been sold, and the transaction cannot be revoked.[35]

What were Pounds' intentions? They did bid for *Vanguard* and indeed Cairnryan was one of the few locations that have could have accommodated the demolition of a ship of her size. She was far too big, of course, for their yard at Portchester. If successful, the work on *Vanguard* would have employed hundreds of locals. Most of the cranes were sold soon after acquisition, but they were not vital for shipbreaking purposes, or in particularly good working order. Having failed to secure *Vanguard*, and without experience of operating a commercial port especially in such a remote location, Pounds realised their investment and moved on.

At the time of writing, it was reported that Pounds still own the lighthouse at Cairnryan.

CHAPTER 5

MOVING TO TIPNER

Purchase of New Premises

Tipner is in Portsmouth harbour, around a mile and a half south of Trafalgar Wharf. As early as 1953, Pounds were granted rights to reclaim a large triangle of the foreshore below the high-water mark there.[36] It was reported later that they were encroaching on War Department land for the storage of scrap metal, adjacent to the triangle. It is not clear whether they had reclaimed the triangle at this stage. Maps prepared in 1964 show no obvious sign of that land having been reclaimed. A 1958 photo confirms Pounds ships moored at Tipner,[37] while records show that business rates were being paid on Tipner land in 1962,

The salvage vessel *Freija* and MTBs *Proud Lancer* and *Proud Highlander* at Tipner, August 1958. Note the concrete blocks onshore, previously used as harbour defences. *(Ian Buxton)*

The Pounds scrapyard at Tipner in 1963. Beyond the oiler *Eddybay* can be seen the Tipner magazine site which was to be bought by Pounds in 1964. This became known as the West Yard. *(Pounds)*

suggesting their occupation was legitimate. The local council were not keen on Pounds' further interest at Tipner, however, and thought of enacting measures preventing shipbreaking activity. It was noted that:

> Pounds [...] have created considerable difficulty for the Corporation with car and ship breaking activities.[38]

In 1964 the adjacent Tipner magazine buildings came up for sale as they were surplus to MOD requirements. The Tipner complex had been opened in 1801 for use by the Royal Navy following acquisition of land there between 1789 and 1791. The risks associated with an accidental explosion causing significant damage were minimised by situating the magazine in this remote corner of Portsmouth harbour. By 1964, the main buildings comprised two magazines (built 1796/8 and 1856) and a cooperage dating from 1798/1800. The buildings were of massive brick construction and their roofs contained sand which would be released in the event of an accidental explosion. The buildings and surrounding plot comprised 4¼ acres of land. Although the pier at Tipner was dilapidated, it did offer valuable deepwater access to Portsmouth harbour, which had not been available at Trafalgar Wharf. Moreover, the Tipner site offered much more space than at the crowded yard at Portchester and was also less conspicuous to passers-by, being situated in a quiet corner of the harbour. Trafalgar Wharf was also attracting interest from the neighbouring Vospers business and was sold to them in 1968.

Tipner – the two massive main magazine buildings in May 2021.

Pounds were to get excellent value from their astute purchase of Tipner. However, at the time, it appeared that they had perhaps paid rather a high price for it at auction on 28 October 1964:

> *There were 30 or 40 people present, including most of the scrap metal dealers, sand and gravel merchants, coal merchants, warehousing concerns, developers, and the like, who had shown interest over recent weeks, but whose type of requirement would apparently be barred by the Planning Authority.*
>
> *[The auctioneer] asked for bids of £40,000, £30,000, and finally £10,000, and then himself raised the bidding to £18,000 before there was a genuine bid. The genuine bidding then went up in thousand-pound jumps to £46,000, £46,500, and finally £47,000. In the early stages there were four bidders, but two soon dropped out.*
>
> *The buyer was Mr H.G. Pounds, scrap metal dealer [...], I might add that this result, about double the most optimistic forecast of the auctioneers, DV and ourselves, was for a property that, although with a total area of 4¼ acres, is largely occupied by old magazines of extremely substantial brick construction with no light or ventilation, and all buildings are in a poor state of repair. The jetty is rotten throughout, and the premises would require very heavy expenditure before being suitable for any use. [...] This is quite apart from the restricted planning which obtains.*[39]

Another commentator concluded:

> *The quite unforeseen outcome of this sale is an example of what sometimes occurs when, despite a property's numerous disadvantages and defects, two wealthy prospective purchasers are determined, for reasons only known to themselves, to buy at whatever may be the cost.*[40]

The magazine buildings are Grade II listed and have retained their original character to this day, though some modifications have been made for modern business use, for example, to allow vehicular access.[41]

The area acquired with the Tipner magazine area became known as Pounds' West Yard. Pounds bought the site through a special-purpose company, Trafalgar Wharves Ltd.[42] With appropriate consent, Pounds reclaimed land beyond the western edge of the West Yard out into Portsmouth harbour. The triangle of land to the east was reclaimed, adding to that part of Pounds estate that became known as the East Yard. Reclamation was done using all manner of material, including rubble from bomb sites in Portsmouth and even concrete blocks from the Skegness harbour defences. Legend has it that surplus tanks and various boats were also used in this process, but Pounds deny this. One unusual ship sacrificed in this cause was the ferro-concrete barge *Eivis*, originally built at Whitby, probably as *RAF 110*. She left the British registry in 1946 and presumably was acquired by Pounds around that time (see photograph on p. 32).

Eivis – an aerial view from May 2025. *(Stephen Wenham)*

A large concrete structure, sometimes referred to as a section of a Mulberry Harbour, was also buried in the East Yard to assist land reclamation. Its origin is unclear.

A modern industrial unit was built in the mid-1970s in the West Yard to house spares and other smaller items of stock. The breaking-up of ships can be a hazardous process for several reasons; fire, for example, cannot always be avoided. Another hazard was arson and vandalism. A newspaper report in 2005 estimated around £2m of damage had been caused to stock and equipment at Tipner over the previous 40 years.[43]

However, in March 1976 the M275 opened, bisecting the Pounds estate and bringing the yard into the public eye. Construction work on the motorway disrupted the Pounds business and there had been occasional brushes with contractors working on the new road. The M275 split the site in two and hindered movement of ships due to the limited headroom imposed by the motorway bridge. Although some compensation was paid, the business was severely affected. Several ships were stranded in the West or East Yard. Before being moved under the motorway bridge, their funnels, superstructure and winching gear had to be removed. One example was HMS *Russell*, seen on the opposite page moving under the motorway in 1985. In addition, the Pounds yard was now visible to passing motorists on the motorway and attracted adverse comments from a small minority. A scrapyard is never likely to provide an attractive view – even if it is a successful, well-organised business. The comments of one county councillor in the press were typical when he stated that the council:

The cut-down hulk of HMS *Russell* eases under the M275 bridge, *c.* 1985. *(R. Allen)*

… should move the shipbreakers out. […] Not only is this place an eyesore but it's also dangerous as drivers take their eyes off the road to look that way. […] Some of the wrecks have been there for years.[44]

Pounds retorted:

Some people build ships; some use them, and other people scrap them. Just what does this journalist think should be done with scrapped ships, unless you are going to put a big plastic sheet over them all? We have been in business for 102 years and were asked to come to this site from Portchester by the City Council in the 1950s. We did so with their blessing but there have been comments like these ever since.[45]

In the 1970s and then from the late 1980s, big efforts were made to clear the East Yard as it had become overcrowded with both ships and piles of military vehicles. Concrete roads had earlier been built around the site to improve business efficiency. One other reason for clearance was the possibility of redevelopment of the area for housing.

People at Pounds

Pounds' new Tipner base was now substantial with the land reclamation proving successful. The East and West Yards were run respectively by 'Old Harry' (Henry George Pounds) and his son 'Young Harry' (Henry Frederick Pounds)

An aerial view of Pounds in about 1980, showing East Yard in foreground and the West Yard beyond the M275. The disruptive effect of the motorway is clear to see. For more aerial views of Tipner, see Chapter 7. (Portsmouth City Museums)

born in 1924. 'Old Harry' focused more on scrap sales whereas 'Young Harry' was keener to resell ships, some of which never came near Pounds' yard. 'Young Harry' was a keen sailor and lived at Tower House, one of Portsmouth's most prestigious properties, enjoying marvellous views on the harbour entrance. 'Old Harry' lived at Boom Tower. His wife Kate kept the records and was influential in the business. The family tree below shows the line of family members who have managed and normally controlled the business. Sometimes 'non-working' family members have owned small parts of the business, but outsiders have never been involved. Pounds has always been family owned and run; moreover a 'hands on' business.

Extracts from the Pounds Family Tree

Frederick Pounds
Baptised Wimborne, 1837
Died Portsea, 1883

Elizabeth Baker
Baptised Luppitt, Devon, 1830
Died Portsea, 1889

Frederick William Pounds (1869–1939)

Florence Exten (1869–1966)

Kate Harriet née Jarmy (1902–99)

Henry George Pounds ('Old Harry') (1897–1971)

Kathleen ('Kass') Pounds (1895–1981)

Bertram Cornish (1892–1971)

Henry Frederick Pounds ('Young Harry') (1924–96)

Mary Margaret Pounds (1931–1997)

Tony Pounds-Cornish (1930–2022)

John Henry Pounds (1955–)

Harry Richard Pounds (1956–)

NB: Family members involved in the business are shown in bold type.

The business has always been run in an efficient manner with costs kept to a minimum; there have never been expensive offices or other extravagant expenditure. Dealings are businesslike and at times may be hard to understand for outsiders unused to the scrap world. For example, in 1978 Pounds were in the news as they won an Admiralty Court case against rival local scrap business Southern Counties Trading Company (owned by the Sullivan family). The dispute concerned ownership of two LCTs, *Abbeville* and *Audemer*. These were both subsequently resold for further commercial use. The judge described 'Young Harry' as:

> *… a tough and ruthless businessman with many of the attributes of a bully in his character. He was prepared to go to great lengths to try to dissuade Mr Sullivan from defending the action.*[46]

One other family member, Young Harry's cousin Tony Pounds-Cornish (1930–2022), was a key figure for over fifty years, working in and later managing the business. Tony went part-time in 2000 before finally retiring in 2003. Tony

'Young Harry' – H.F. Pounds
(1924–96). (Pounds)

Roger Allen pictured with the propeller of *Russell*.
(R.Allen)

recounted to the author many interesting stories about his working life at Pounds. One told of how, aged 17 or so, he was sent to Beirut by 'Old Harry' to bid in an auction of military surplus. Rather terrified at the prospect, he actually found that, on hearing he was from Pounds, the other attendees treated him with enormous respect and he was given a prominent position.

Another key employee was Roy Hazzard who joined the business as a 16-year-old in the 1930s, initially acting as a chauffeur for 'Old Harry'. During the Second World War, Roy served in the Army as a tank driver and was involved in many campaigns, including Normandy. Roy was to be involved in the Pounds business for around sixty years until 1993. He was one of a small number of important and trusted employees. Others were Wilf Blaimer and Nigel Ince, who started at Pounds in 1974. Commander John Rayner, an ex-submariner, joined the business after the war and became yard manager in the 1980s. Dave McDermott (1952–2022) managed the yard from the late 1990s, having joined the business as a driver in 1967. Contractors have on occasions been involved, usually for specific tasks.

One such example was the need to clear much of the East Yard following the death of 'Old Harry' in 1971. With this in mind, 'Young Harry' engaged Sid Dean (1930–2020) as a contractor. Sid had valuable experience, having worked in the Metrec scrap and salvage business at Newhaven. Dean would buy an area of scrap in the East Yard from Pounds, cut it up and then sell it to third parties. Dean put up £10,000 as an advance payment for the scrap he was to clear, a considerable amount at the time, as he recalled. Dean worked for five years or so in the East Yard, clearing other military vehicles; he estimated that fifty Sherman tanks and fifty Bren Gun carriers and as well as tugs, the submarine *Statesman*, minesweepers and smaller vessels were dismantled during this time. Dean was assisted by his sons Philip and John as well as two employees and in all estimates that he cleared at least 1,000 tons of scrap; likely the true figure was much more.

Another contractor, Roger Allen (1941–2024), joined Pounds from Willments shipyard in 1978 and was to work in the business for nineteen years. He also bought hulks from Pounds which he demolished on his own account.

Sid Dean in 2019.

The current Harry Pounds
(1956–). *(Pounds)*

Tony Pounds-Cornish in 2011.
(G. Pounds-Cornish)

The crowded East Yard in the 1970s at the time that Sid Dean was clearing much of
Old Harry's stock. In the centre, two *TID* tugs can be seen in the middle distance.
Bassingham is to the left and the funnel of *Bold Pathfinder* is just visible. *(Pounds)*

One example in 1985 was the frigate HMS *Russell*, which needed to be cut down
and lightened in order to be towed under the M275 with a reported 18 inches
to spare (see photo on p. 33)!

In 1996 Young Harry died following an accident at home and was buried
at sea. His son, another Harry Pounds, took over the business and ran it
efficiently until closure in 2023.

Purchases of Ships

Although Pounds are quite often referred to as shipbreakers, their main activity, besides scrap and the demolition of army vehicles,[47] was usually trading in ships, particularly under Young Harry. The list of nearly 600 ships bought by Pounds (which can be found in Appendix 2) confirms that around two-thirds of them were resold for further commercial use, rather than being scrapped. Such disposals were made using the business's outstanding range of contacts worldwide. Sales of ships or the resale of their equipment would usually be a far more profitable operation than demolition. Table 1 shows the predominance of ship trading as opposed to shipbreaking.

Table 1. Fate of Ships Bought 1921–2023

Period of Acquisition	Total Ships Bought in Period	Broken Up by Pounds	Resold for Further Service	Resold to other Breakers	Unknown
1921–9	25	10	3	1	11
1930–9	5	0	2	0	3
1940–9	43	3	7	0	33
1950–9	70	6	27	3	34
1960–9	128	9	61	20	38
1970–9	139	13	53	25	48
1980–9	74	5	46	6	17
1990–9	72	10	40	3	19
2000–9	14	6	3	0	5
2010–23	18	10	6	0	2
Total	**588**	**72**	**248**	**58**	**210**

Smaller ships, such as inshore minesweepers and tugs, were particularly suitable for resale. Minesweepers may not have been expensive to buy as being largely made of wood, the potential yield from recycling is not great. Tugs are durable and often have exceptionally long working lives. Landing craft were also often resold, thousands had been built in the Second World War and were available at low prices. These could usually be resold for commercial use, sometimes after modification. Table 2 shows that these ship types were strong candidates for purchase, mainly due to the resale possibilities.

Table 2. Selected Ship Types Bought 1921–2023

Ship Type	Number Bought
Tugs	106
Minesweepers	60
Landing craft	27
Dredgers	24
Submarines	21
Trawlers	22
Ferries	14

Besides the outright purchase of ships and vehicles, Pounds were able to deploy their expertise in such diverse projects as removing wartime submarine defences off Southsea and some at Scapa Flow. At Skegness, the old concrete sea defences were removed and recycled for use in both marinas as yacht moorings around the UK and for land reclamation at Tipner. There have been offbeat customers too, for example, the Aspinall Wild Animal Parks at Howletts and Port Lympne in Kent bought ropes for their gorillas and monkeys to swing from!

Pounds were not greatly affected by fluctuations in the fortunes of the rest of the British shipbreaking industry, which had drastically reduced in size by the late 1980s. As can be seen in Table 1, most of the ships they purchased were resold for further commercial service. Also, Pounds' interest has always been in smaller ships (most under 1,000grt) and transportation costs made such vessels unattractive to potential overseas shipbreakers. Pounds were at no time members of the British Shipbreakers Association, neither were they on the list of ships allocated by the British Iron & Steel Corporation (Salvage) Ltd (BISCO) for demolition.[48]

Most ships would be acquired by competitive tender, and it was vital to assess likely quantities of metals and reusable equipment (and possible resale value) to determine a bid price for each vessel. This was not too difficult for Pounds as quite often they would buy several ships of the same class or type. For example, they acquired as many as twenty-two Ham class inshore minesweepers, although admittedly the three types of Ham had differing quantities of valuable non-ferrous metals.

All ships, once purchased, would be surveyed to check for major defects and whether they could be safely towed to Pounds. Ernest Wilson performed this crucial function for Pounds for many years. It was also necessary to assess the quantities of metals and reusable equipment in order to estimate a tender price for the vessel in the first instance. A typical report by Wilson is shown on the left.

The detailed purchasing strategy of the business is discussed overleaf.

Many ships were acquired and, in many cases, they remained in the yard for prolonged periods. They could be sold or scrapped depending on market conditions or the

ERNEST C. WILSON
C. Eng., F.R.I.N.A., F.I.Mar.E.

Naval Architect and Surveyor
Gravesend 0474 534029

48 PINE AVENUE,
GRAVESEND,
KENT DA12 1QZ

TOWAGE CERTIFICATE

Pounds Marine & Shipping Ltd.,
49 Bedhampton Lane,
Havant, Hants

SURVEY REPORT No. 3422

DATE 22nd. July 1991

REPORT OF SURVEY

THIS IS TO CERTIFY that the undersigned Surveyor

did at the request of Messrs. Pounds Marine and Shipping Ltd., of 49 Bedhampton Lane, Havant, Hants did examine whilst afloat four Trinity House light vessels Nos.3-11-12 & 23 at Harwich. These lightships had recently come off station and all are in a sound and seaworthy condition and have been efficiently closed up. All seacocks closed, vents sealed as necessary and the vessels are ready to be towed from Harwich to Portsmouth by the motor tug "TOWING CHIEFTAIN" in reasonable weather conditions and in WINDS UP TO FORCE FIVE [max wind speed 20 mph].

TOWAGE:-The towage is being undertaken by Lloyds approved towage contractor Messrs T.S.A.Tugs Ltd.,of 106 Tattersal Gardens. Leigh on Sea, Essex,SS9 9QZ with their motor tug "TOWING CHIEFTAIN" having the following particulars:-
Length.............29.9 metres
Beam.............. 7.8 "
Draft............. 3.8 "
Bollard Pull..... 24.00 tons
ENGINES:-Two M.A.N.diesel units 800 BHP coupled to L&S gearbox, single shaft to V.P. propeller.

TOWING AREANGEMENTS:- The following towing arrangements were discussed with the owners and are approved.
The lightships are to be towed in pairs.
Each lightship has a 26mm high tensile stud link chain bridle secured to the forward bitts lugs 15 metres long, one vessels chain bridle shackled to thw towing winch wire 38mm circ. the second vessel has a similar chain bridle shackled to 8" circ nylon towing hawser 150 metres long attached to the tugs towing hook.
Navigation lights to D.O.T and emergency towing hawsers to be fitted to each vessel with buoyed trailing lines attached.
The vessels being practically identical the "TOWING CHIEFTAIN" will make two trips towing the vessels as detailed in the aforegoing

TOWING CONDITIONS:-The master of the "TOWING CHIEFTAIN" Capt. Marcel le Comte to check that the weather forecast covering the duration of the tow are within the limits imposed above before commencing the tow so as to ensure the safe arrival of the four lightships at Portsmouth.

The lightships Nos .3 -11 -12 and 23 any two of he four listed can be towed by the "TOWING CHIEFTAIN at one time.

Bold Pathfinder awaiting final break-up in the East Yard, 1985. *(R. Allen)*

receipt of a good offer. Demolition might occur only after a long spell at Pounds. An example was the fast patrol boat *Bold Pathfinder*. Bought in 1962, she was resold to a firm in Naples which extracted her valuable diesel engines and gas turbines and sold the hulk back to Pounds in 1966. She was to linger in the yard until March 1985 when a rise in aluminium prices prompted her final demolition.

Quite often, ships that could not be resold were sold to other breakers, particularly in Belgium and the Netherlands, for scrapping. Space was limited for demolition in Pounds' yards and the Low Countries were not far away. Willments in nearby Southampton was one of several UK breakers which regularly took ships from Pounds.

A couple of unusual purchases are covered next, before a review of specific ship types purchased.

The Victorian Gunboat *Demon*

In early 1972 *Demon* was bought for a modest £1,240 from the Dover Harbour Board, where she has been used as a crane barge. There was little interest in maritime circles in her long-term conservation, and she has now sadly been dismantled.

Launched as the trials gunboat *Handy* by C. Mitchell & Co. on the Tyne in December 1882, she was iron hulled. Bought by the Royal Navy in 1883, she was sent to the Whale Island gunnery school in 1891 where she was renamed

Excellent. She was part of Admiral Hood's force, which bombarded the Belgian coast in 1914. Relegated to reserve shortly afterwards, she was sold to the Dover Harbour Board in 1922 and they renamed her *Demon.* She was refitted as a crane barge with a crane fitted in place of her massive gun turret.

In July 2002 *Navy News* contrasted *Demon*'s plight with that of one of her contemporaries, the naval sloop HMS *Gannet,* which had been built in 1878. Preserved at the Chatham Historic Dockyard, *Gannet* has been fortunate to have been allocated £3m of funding from the Heritage Lottery Fund. *Navy News* described *Demon*'s condition as 'rough but recoverable... the decks need attention and there is still structural work to be done'.

Demon in April 2005.

Above: *Demon* at Dover (as *Snapper*), *c.* 1930. Note the 25-ton crane carried by her. *(Andrew Humphreys collection)*

Right: Pounds had plans to restore *Demon* themselves and for this purpose, purchased a Vavasseur gun in the 1990s.

An evocative image of *Demon* at Dover. *(Author's collection)*

Demon at Dover in the 1960s. *(John Hendy collection)*

HMS *Volage*

Arriving at Pounds in 1973, this Type 15 frigate spent three years in the West Yard before any work at all was done on her. She was one of several Royal Navy ships acquired around this time by Pounds for which there was no prospect of resale for further service; quite simply, this was not permitted by the MOD. The two others were the submarines *Tiptoe* (1971) and *Artemis* (1972). The three vessels cost around £89,000 in total, a significant investment and one that took quite a while to realise as all three were only finally broken up in the early 1990s. In part, their acquisition may have been prompted by the fact that the larger shipbreakers, such as T.W. Ward, were preoccupied with tankers which were becoming available on the world market at particularly low prices. Also, small breakers such as Pounds could undercut them, owing to their lower overheads.

Pounds only had permission to break *Volage* up in the East Yard but in the meantime the M275 had been built across the yard, causing great inconvenience. To facilitate relocation to the East Yard, she was cut down by a crane lighter (ex-LBK) *YC 3029* and in February 1979 her hulk was refloated and moved carefully under the motorway bridge. She was beached in the East Yard and then hauled further up on the shore in August 1979 to prevent the channel becoming blocked. Over the next few years, the hulk was cut up by contractor George Smith and had all but disappeared by the late 1980s. However, as we go to press, remnants of *Volage* can still be seen at low tide.

A listing *Volage*, 1975.
(*Stephen Wenham*)

A tranquil scene in December 1975 as *Volage* awaits her fate. She is seen here along with (from left) 90ft MFV, *Rackham*, and an ex-RAF 68ft rescue/target-towing launch. (*WSS Photo Library, James Goss collection, hereafter 'Goss'*)

Above: By August 1979, *Volage* (second left) was in the East Yard and well cut down, flanked on the left by the submarine *Tiptoe* and on the right by the crane barge *C21*. *(Goss)*

Opposite: Remnants of the stern of *Volage* at Tipner, May 2025. *(Stephen Wenham)*

Below: A twin 40mm Mark V Bofors gun, probably from *Volage*, was still in the yard in July 2006. *(Ian Buxton)*

Landing Craft

Landing craft can often be resold profitably for commercial use, sometimes with little or no modification. Examples of such purchases immediately after 1945 have been discussed above.

One interesting aspect of the *Audemer* court case mentioned earlier in this chapter is the revelation of the profits to be made by astute reselling of these craft. The two LCTs were bought for £88,367 but there seemed a ready prospect of them being resold for £325,000 (US$400,000).

An earlier example was the LCT (8) *Citadel*, which was sold on by Pounds for £18,076 in 1971, despite being heavily corroded and having been poorly maintained at Chatham. Large shipbreaker, Shipbreaking Industries (SI) were outbid by Pounds as, in determining their offer, SI had estimated that the market value of the ship was its scrap value of just £4,481.[49]

Later, in 1975, a rare Landing Craft Flak (LCF) *34* was acquired from D.S. Vernon, scrap dealers of Chichester. She was laid up in the East Yard until hopes for preservation faded and she was demolished around 1990. LCFs were landing craft with their bow doors welded up and carrying a formidable gun armament. Only forty-six were built in all, so LCF *34* was probably the last survivor of this type. LCF *34* served on D-Day as part of Assault Group S3. By October 1944 she was in 'pooled reserve' and was originally acquired by Vernons in 1946.

Krokodil and her half-sister *Eidechse* were bought from the West German Navy and were both ex-US LSMs. They were both sold on to Ocean Offshore Services, Guernsey, for further commercial service. Pounds acquired several vessels from the US Navy in 1975/6. One of the biggest of these was an LCT believed to be called *Texas*, bought for £49,089 in July 1975 and reported to have been resold for commercial use in March 1976.

In 1977, Pounds also acquired the ex-US LSM *Hjaelperen*. She had been converted to a torpedo boat tender before being transferred to the Royal Danish Navy. She was resold by Pounds for breaking up at Willments, Southampton, on the River Itchen.

Topmast 18 (pictured on p. 48) was a former Landing Craft Tank (LCT) Mark 3 completed in 1942. Acquired by Pounds, she was then sold in September 1965 for £16,500 to leading salvage company Risdon Beazley, who expertly converted her for their work. Her tank decks were transformed into accommodation and a cargo hold capable of carrying 350 to 400 tons. Extensive equipment was fitted on deck, including a grabbing derrick capable of lifting 10 tons. Risdon Beazley were adept at skilled wreck clearance not involving explosives, and would look to make a full recovery of a ship's cargo. Pounds acquired her again from Beazley in December 1976 for £19,500 and her bright appearance (Risdon Beazley colours) stood out amid the grey of the other ships in the yard. Pounds were fitting her out for further commercial service, but this work was halted by a fire in June 1978. No further work was done on her and the hulk was sold to shipbreakers Bakkers in Bruges in 1984 for demolition.

Her identical sister-ship *Topmast 20*, former *LCT 399* (Mark 3) converted by Risdon Beazley, was seen on Pounds' moorings and having been sold on for future commercial use as *Recovery*, was broken up at Grimsby in 1991.

LCF *34* in September 1989, to the far left the hulk of *P556*. (*T.W. Ferrers-Walker*)

This view shows LCF *34* and the submarine *P556* on the foreshore of the East Yard, May 1978. (*After the Battle* magazine)

Another LCT, *Bastion*. Note dilapidated old magazine jetty and several Ton class minesweepers to the right. (*Jack Smale*)

Krokodil at Pounds. (*Drawing by Barry Robertson*)

Hjaelperen cut down
at Willments,
7 September 1982.
(Ian Buxton)

Topmast 18 and *Audemer*,
May 1979.
(Keith Miller)

The Danish landing
craft *Tyr*, which was
refurbished and then
resold in 1970.
(Pounds)

Surplus from Portsmouth Dockyard

Pounds have always worked closely with the Royal Dockyard at Portsmouth, which is located nearby. Sometimes vessels were in such poor condition (for example, the frigate HMS *Russell* in 1985) that they could only really be safely towed locally to Pounds. A low price would be obtained by Pounds in such cases. Pounds were willing to assist in clearing obsolete and other unwanted material from the Dockyard and in the 1950s this had included some timbers from HMS *Victory*, Nelson's flagship. Surplus 12- and 14-inch shells were acquired in the 1960s after the explosive had been removed.

Most commonly, small dockyard craft were bought by Pounds, who could see a viable use for them and could thus resell for further service, often at a good profit. Armament carriers were one such type.

On other occasions, yard craft were used in the business. YC 3029, for example, a former LBK, was deployed in the demolition of *Volage*. Once the 'flat iron' Victorian gunboat *Fidget* (1872), C21 had worked at Portsmouth Dockyard since 1905 and was fitted out by Pounds as a crane barge following purchase in 1964.

As highlighted, proximity to Portsmouth Dockyard certainly facilitated Pounds' purchase of ships that were damaged and possibly in too poor a condition to be towed safely elsewhere. The three inshore minesweepers *Bisham*, *Broadley* and *Edlingham* were damaged in a catastrophic fire in the harbour in September 1956 and bought by Pounds, who did not demolish them until the 1980s. The three had been laid up together for long-term preservation, in a similar fashion to the four shown at the foot of p. 57.

Redundant US ships were acquired from the nearby military port of Marchwood in the Solent, with examples including tugs, the giant LARC amphibious craft and more recently the *Apache* crane.

Away from Portsmouth, in 1962 Pounds acquired the unusual floating dock at Penarth in South Wales. Built in 1909 by Swan, Hunter & Wigham Richardson, the L-shaped structure had become redundant following closure of the docks. It is unclear whether Pounds intended to scrap this in situ or take her away by sea for possible onward sale. Certain difficulties arose, leading to the dock sinking and blocking the harbour. A court case ensued involving Pounds, heard before the illustrious Lord Denning. The harbour company were awarded £750 or so in damages (see photographs on p. 58).

Armament carriers *NA1* and *NA46*, bought by Pounds in 1955 and 1970 respectively. *(Pounds)*

Above: *Bowstring*, another armament carrier, December 1984. She was eventually resold for scrap. (The News)

Left: The hopper barge *W33 Minhop3* arrived at Tipner in 1969. *(Pounds)*

Opposite above: *C158* was originally a dumb oil fuel lighter built in 1905. The crane and propeller suggest a new use, probably after her sale by RMAS to Belsize Yard, Southampton, in 1962, who then presumably sold her on to Pounds. She is seen here at end of the Tipner jetty. *(Pounds)*

Opposite below: *C21* for many years served as a crane barge around Pounds. She had been a lighter with the Fleet Fuelling Service when Pounds bought her in 1964. *(Jack Smale)*

YC 477 was a dumb cooking lighter, serving principally at Devonport. Bought by Pounds in 1982, she is seen here in 1985 at Tipner. The vessel is believed to have been resold for commercial service on a fish farm in the Shetlands. *(Author's collection)*

Trials vessel *Whimbrel*, a Naval Stores tender (foreground), and *Fordham*, April 1989. *(P. Simons)*

Naval surplus of all types made their way to Pounds. Seen here in March 1995 is an Admiralty Salvage Pontoon (*ASP 15*), not used very much nowadays.

Assorted debris in a corner of the yard in 2006, possibly including tubular remnants of a *Chariot* submarine. *(Ian Buxton)*

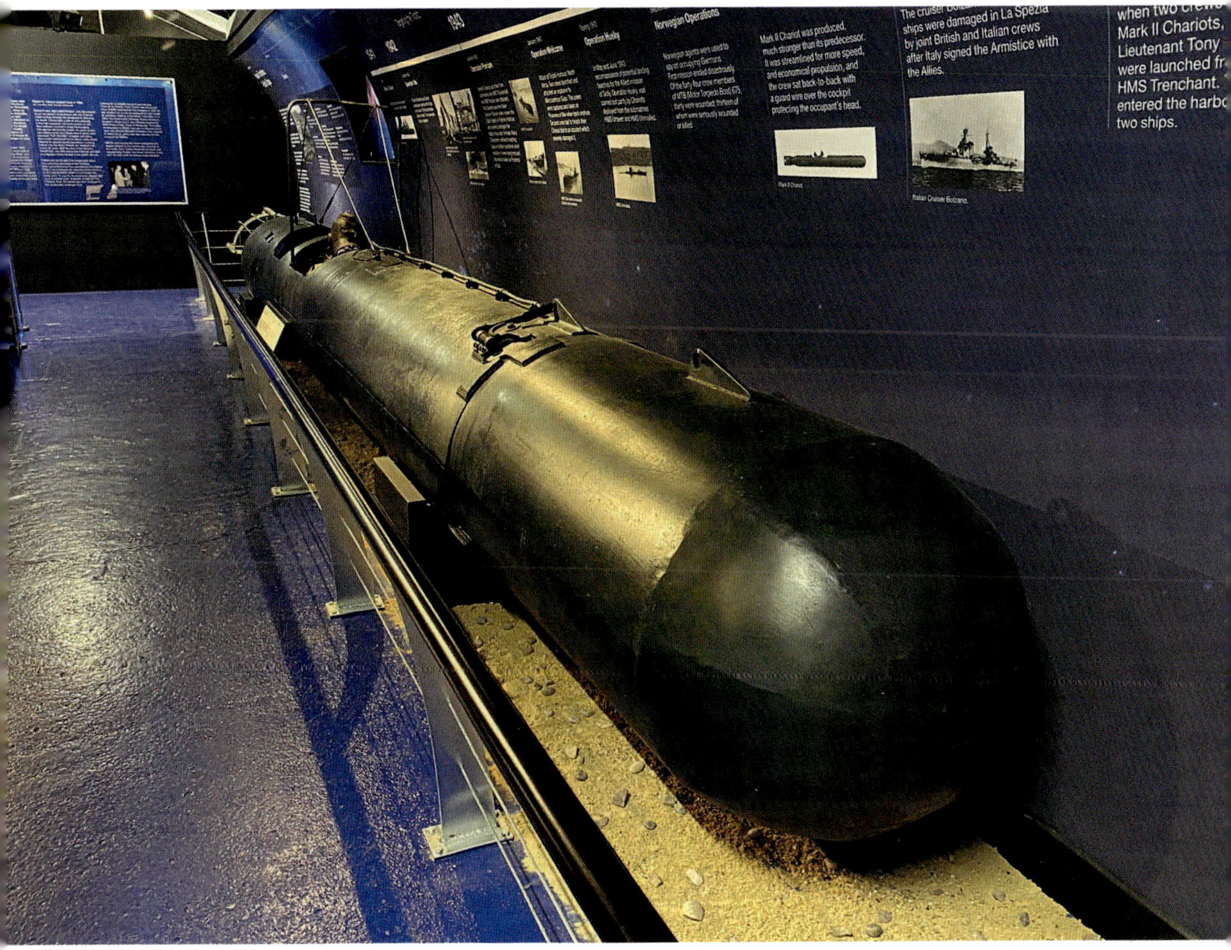

'Human torpedo' ('Chariot' Mark 2) acquired from Pounds, *c.* 1998. Following restoration, this is now on display at Eden Camp Modern History Museum, Yorkshire. *(Eden Camp photo)*

RNAL 50 carrying Sea Vixen aircraft, 1966. Aircraft lighters like *RNAL 50* would ferry aircraft to and from aircraft carriers. Later in their careers they became 'dummy decks', used to train helicopter pilots and deck crews. *(Ian Buxton)*

RNAL 50 on Pounds moorings, being used for storage, 2013. *(Jeremy Shaw)*

An ex-LCT (3), Maintenance and Repair Craft (MRC) *1015*, bought by Pounds in 1965. *(Pounds)*

14-inch (left) and 12-inch naval shells formerly used
in gun trials, pictured in 1991.

Practice 21-inch torpedoes. *(Ian Buxton)*

An anchor, possibly of similar vintage to the early nineteenth-century Tipner magazine building seen in the background of this 2005 view.

Yet more surplus from Portsmouth dockyard. Anchors of varying ages are pictured here in July 1999.

To the left of this photograph is a caisson (possibly a C/D lock spare), formerly in Portsmouth dockyard. On the right can be seen the submarine HMS *Oracle*, alongside the deteriorating old magazine jetty, 2002.

The former Red Funnel pontoon from Cowes, Isle of Wight, for the fast ferry service. Its fate is unknown, but quite possibly it was resold.

Two semi-automatic 4.5-inch turrets were acquired from the RN Gunnery School at Whale Island. *(Pounds)*
On the right is one that remained at Pounds until the yard was cleared in 2023. The other was transferred
to the Explosion Museum of Naval Firepower, Priddy's Hard, where it can be seen today.

The three burnt-out minesweepers, *Broadley*, *Edlingham* and *Bisham*, at Pounds yard, Tipner, 1958. *(Ian Buxton)*

Four inshore minesweepers laid up, May 1955. *Bucklesham* is seen nearest the camera. *(The News)*

Above: The Penarth floating dock on completion in 1909.
(*Author's collection*)

A 1911 image of the sailing ship *Alster* on the Penarth floating dock. (*Author's collection*)

Purchases from around Portsmouth Harbour

One unusual acquisition was the huge coal hulk *C1*, built by Swan, Hunter & Wigham Richardson and completed in 1904. Soon after, she went into service in Portsmouth harbour as a floating coal yard for the then coal-fired fleet. She had a huge capacity for 11,000 tons of coal in hoppers and 1,080 tons in bags, making her the biggest of her type in the world. She was especially busy during the First World War, surviving in this role until bought by Pounds in September 1963 and quickly sold on for breaking in the Netherlands. Her function had reduced and eventually became obsolete as the use of coal by the Royal Navy diminished (see photograph on p. 60).[50]

Pounds were in a good position to acquire unwanted hulks or ships – an example in 1985 was *Black Prince*, the former RN trials pontoon *Sarepta II*. She had previously been parked by her owner in Portchester Lake, adjacent to his houseboat, to function as a breakwater and for storage and use in their furniture restoring business. This ceased when Portsmouth County Court ordered her removal, leading to Pounds' acquisition. She was cut in two by them with one half being sold as a pontoon and the other half scrapped.

Sometimes hulks emanated from local mercantile use – for example, the former French barge *Bressuire* was bought by Pounds in 1981 and resold for breaking in Belgium. Built in 1918, she had served since 1953 in Portsmouth harbour initially as a coal hulk and then, once the last coal-fired ferry *Ryde* was taken out of service in 1969, as a mooring station for out-of-service Sealink ferries. Her stern was painted blaze orange to stand out in the often-crowded harbour. She was sold in 1981 as her hull plates were deteriorating. Pounds had also bought *Bressuire*'s predecessor coal hulk *C11* in 1953 and resold her to British Railways for further use.

Bressuire with the ferry *Brading* and RFA *Olmeda* behind her. (The News)

Coal hulk *C1*. *(Pounds)*

Black Prince at Portchester.
(The News)

Ferries

Many Isle of Wight ferries were bought by Pounds, but several were purchased from other locations. One Isle of Wight ferry bought was *Freshwater*, which was to be resold as *Sound of Seil* for further service in West Scotland. Press rumours that she was to be sold as a landing craft for Beirut militia therefore proved unfounded! She ended her days at the Garston scrapyard on the Mersey in 1997.

Later, another Isle of Wight ferry – *Brading* – was acquired, and to facilitate breaking, she was set alight in November 1994 in a controlled fire. Although the fire was under control, the local fire brigade were alerted and hundreds of locals watched the blaze. A controlled fire enables valuable non-ferrous metals to be exposed and extracted easily; the burning of low-value timber is an acceptable price to pay for this.

The opening of the Tay Road Bridge in August 1966 made three ferries redundant and two were bought by Pounds to be sold for further service in Malta.

Freshwater in the West Yard in September 1984. Alongside is the degaussing vessel *Warmingham* and an unidentified 43ft Naval Stores tender. *(Pounds)*

A closer view of *Freshwater.* (The News)

Brading (right) rusting away prior to demolition. *Afan* is seen alongside.

Brading being demolished in the West Yard, her funnel gone. *(Pounds)*

One of the Tay ferries, *Scotscraig. (Pounds)*

Repton's bridge structure and engine ashore, alongside the area leased out as an aggregates yard. *(R. Allen)*

Minesweepers

These were frequent acquisitions by Pounds, sixty-seven in all. One example was the fourteen Ton class coastal minesweepers acquired, mainly between 1968 and 1977. Only two are known to have been demolished at Tipner and at least nine of the others were sold for scrapping at other breakers, possibly after Pounds had stripped them of their valuable non-ferrous metals. None appear to have been resold for commercial service.

In contrast to the Tons, many smaller inshore minesweepers were often resold for further use, often as pleasure craft for which they were highly suitable. Conversions were also easier due to their features, including an open deck. Pounds bought twenty-two Ham class inshore minesweepers, mainly between 1966 and 1983. One or two are still serving as tour vessels in the Mediterranean.

Inshore minesweepers were also bought from the US Navy, having been lent post-war to various European navies and not needed back in the USA. Others bought had no apparent US connection, such as the Italian inshore minesweepers *Arsella* and *Conchiglia* (see p. 95), which were of a similar design to the Ham class.

Above: HMS *Leverton* flanked by another Ton class vessel in December 1975. She was resold in 1977 for breaking up at Willments at Southampton. *(Goss)*

Opposite above: Several Tons were bought in the early 1970s and the enclosed bridges on two reveal them to be probably (from left) *Fiskerton, Leverton* and *Puncheston*, alongside *TCC Hopper No 3* in this 1974 view. *Fiskerton* and *Puncheston* were resold in 1977 for demolition at Dartford. The *Hopper* was sold for further commercial service. *(Jack Smale)*

Opposite middle: The largest minesweeper bought by Pounds was the Portuguese *São Jorge*, bought from A.F. Ross and Sons, who had previously laid her up at Cairnryan. Arriving at Tipner in February 1979, she was broken up within nine months. An ex-US Navy ship (USS *MSO 478*), she was a rare purchase by Pounds of an oceangoing minesweeper. *(Keith Miller)*

Opposite below: *Sheraton* pictured in July 1999, one of the few Tons broken up by Pounds. She was bought with her sister *Brinton* for a combined cost of nearly £104,000 in 1997.

Many Tons were sold for breaking elsewhere. One example was *Nurton*, shown here being cut up at the former Cochrane shipbuilders yard at Selby by Dawn Premier Services, *c*. 1995. *(Steven Tacey)*

Final stages of break-up of *Sheraton* November 2000, showing engine room, forward bulkhead and the main engine seatings.

The stern sections of *Sheraton*.

This internal view of *Sheraton* shows the utilitarian 1950s décor and furnishings.

The engine is being removed from *Dittisham* in this 1997 view.

Rackham in a crowded scene in the East Yard. In the background, among others, are *P556* and the blue-hulled *Lune Venture* ex-*MFV 1562*. *(C. Duncan)*

Four Hams sold for further service as pleasure craft in Corfu. Left to right: *Petrakis I* (ex-*Thatcham*), *Sotirakis I* (ex-*Sandringham*), *Sotirakis* (ex-*R.G. Masters*) and *Petrakis* (ex-*Thakeham*). *(Pounds)*

Tongham, pictured with *Medway Queen* at Gillingham, August 2023. *Tongham* was most recently used as a café after spending many years as a houseboat.

Above right: Many Ham class minesweepers were later modified for specialist use. *Fordham* (pictured here) had been deployed for degaussing work and was sold to Pounds in 1980. Several Hams were sold for further commercial service, but some, like *Fordham*, were stripped for spares, prior to the hulk being broken up. *(Fricker)*

Shipham in the West Yard in 1991. She was to be broken up after 1995, maybe as her stern had been severely damaged in a collision in 1985 with a buoy off Felixstowe, making a resale for further service problematic.

Many ships surplus to requirements, including minesweepers, were bought from the US Navy in the mid-1970s. Some had been lent post-1945 to friendly European navies. *(Pounds)*

Tugs

A large number of tugs were bought, and a few were used by Pounds for towing and moving ships around the yard. Examples were *Towing Wizard* (1971–8), *Lord Ritchie* (1977–85) and *Metheringham*. Many other tugs – which usually have long working lives – were resold for further use.

Above: Swansea tug *Kendiken*, acquired *c.* 1972 and resold for further service. *(Lennon)*

Opposite above: *TID 32*, one of twelve *TID* small tugs bought by Pounds, is seen here in June 1972 and was broken up in about 1976. *(The late P.A. Vicary collection)*

Opposite below: The East Yard in the early 1970s with several tugs, including *TID 50*. Just visible to rear is the fin of former US submarine *P556*. *(Jack Smale)*

Below: *Lord Ritchie* was bought by Pounds in 1976 to be used as the yard tug, and was involved in filming of *The Greek Tycoon*. Later she was sold on to Cleanaway in 1985 and renamed *Jim Higgs*. *(Author's collection)*

Miscellaneous Purchases

Trawlers were not bought often by Pounds so a particularly surprising arrival in 1969 was a group of nine East German trawlers, accompanied by a mother ship which then left them at Pounds moorings. With the Cold War at its height, the purchase was even more unusual. Their crews did not have the appropriate papers so were detained briefly by immigration authorities and then repatriated to East Berlin, for which they in fact already had tickets. Ten stayed on their trawler *Karl Liebknecht*, hoping for asylum, but were also put on flights home by the UK immigration authorities.

Only five other trawler purchases have been traced, two of which are illustrated on p. 73.

Frequently, ships would be bought by Pounds and then resold quickly for further service and less often for demolition. The onward sale no doubt was often lined up before the purchase was even made. On many of these transactions, the ships in question would not come to Portsmouth harbour but be sold where they lay. An example, and indeed one of Pounds' biggest purchases, was the *Salisbury* (1944/6108) damaged and lying in the Seychelles. Bought in 1970 via the Crown Agents for US$120,880, she was resold for breaking in Singapore in 1971, without coming to the UK.

Occasionally elderly hovercraft would be bought from local operators and usually scrapped.

On other occasions, ships would be conveyed to Pounds' moorings in Portsmouth harbour and resold without coming into the yard. One example was the *Weather Surveyor*, bought by Pounds in 1977 for £25,380, and laid up on their moorings until 1983 when a surge in scrap prices resulted in a sale to Dutch breakers for £50,000. Built as the frigate HMS *Rushen Castle*, she was converted to a weather ship at Blyth in 1961.

Another weather ship, *Weather Observer* (ex-Flower class corvette HMS *Marguerite*), was purchased in 1961 and quickly sold on to Van Heyghen Frères (VHF), the breakers in Ghent.

Colliers were bought from time to time. One of these was *Pompey Light*, bought in 1966 but sent to breakers in Antwerp in 1968 as presumably there was no prospect of a profitable resale for further commercial use.

Weather Surveyor on Pounds' moorings, April 1981. *(Jeremy Shaw)*

Pintail and *249A* are seen in this November 1991 picture. *Pintail* was launched in 1963 at Cammel Laird Birkenhead; she could assist in the maintenance of the heaviest moorings as well as salvage and maintaining booms for harbour defence.

Joe Croan and *Mount Everest*, trawlers bought in 1977 for a total of £30,000. *(Lennon)*

The cockpit of the *Idun Viking* hovercraft is seen here in 2017. It was sold to a private buyer who donated it to the Southampton Hall of Aviation. The rest of the hovercraft had already been scrapped before Pounds acquired her. *(Stephen Wenham)*

Pompey Light in service. *(Pounds)*

Historic Vessels

Pounds, on occasions, were glad to acquire historic vessels and hold them in their yard, with a view to promoting their long-term preservation. *LCF 34* is a case in point and is discussed on pp. 46–47.

Sometimes Pounds' moorings would offer a safe haven for ships of this type. One example is the large side trawler *Ross Revenge*, which arrived in February 1980. She was owned by a business associate of Pounds, Captain Silas Oates. Shortly afterwards after moving on to Cairnryan for demolition, the *Ross Revenge* was rescued by Radio Caroline and refitted in Spain as their radio ship, a role she incredibly still fulfils as we go to press in 2025.

Other ships allowed time on Pounds' moorings while rescue efforts were made included the ferry *Southsea* (sister of *Brading*) but unfortunately she ended up being scrapped in Denmark. The LST *Stalker* (see p. 95) was scrapped at Pounds after rescue efforts over several years failed.

Completed in February 1944 at Gosport, *MFV 119* was immediately allocated to US forces and served on D-Day at Omaha Beach. She later took supplies to Le Havre for the US Army. She was used a diving tender from 1978 by the Royal Navy and Royal Marines Sub Aqua Club on wrecks such as *Invincible* (1758). After this interesting role ceased, she was laid up in No 2 Basin, Portsmouth, not in the best of states. Apparently, she needed daily attention to be kept afloat. She was rescued from this precarious state by Pounds. Eventually she went to Isle of Wight owners who restored and modernised her and she has been available since 2019 as a holiday let at East Cowes Marina (see p. 76).

The cable ship *St Margarets*, completed in 1944, arrived at Pounds in November 1985. A reporter from the local paper was lucky to tour her:

Once she was a proud old lady of the sea. Now her distinct black and buff colours still clearly visible, the cable ship St Margarets *lies in Pounds scrapyard Tipner, the resting place of many a brave ship. Pensioned off in 1984, she was the last steam-reciprocating vessel in naval service, a friendly lady who gave her best to the last and was known affectionately to her crew as Maggie. Her interior belonged to another era with its lovely wood panelling (now painted) and gleaming brass. Those who knew her miss her small but welcoming wardroom. The bar, which used to be full of shining bottles (they never lasted long enough to collect dust) was at the far end surrounded by comfortable armchairs. The officers' cabins were situated along a single alley way, which ran through the centre of the ship and was open at either end. They all had louvered doors, an attractive feature reminiscent of past Empire building days. They were more suited to warm climates than to the North Atlantic where she had spent most of her twilight days. The captain's accommodation was [...] fitted with magnificent mahogany panelling all round; it had the heavy luxury of a bygone age. In contrast the crew's quarters lacked any modicum of comfort or convenience so much so that extra pay was awarded for putting up with its discomfort. [...] Her engines were a steam enthusiast's dream. They too were full of highly polished wood and gleaming brass. Everything on board from cable winches to bilge pumps was run on*

steam. Being a very sensitive power source, steam was ideal for the minute and exact work demanded by cable laying. […] The boiler room was some distance from the engine room and was pressurised when she was under way. This meant that anyone going in or out had to pass through an airlock […]

The cabling gear was also driven by steam. It was fitted to the foredeck with engines, which were miniature versions of the main ship's engine and each cable drum was fitted with brakes, which had lignum vitae shoes […] the problem that finally brought about her demise was that her boiler tubes had wasted away over the years. Repairing these was no longer economically viable […] she was a ship which demanded a lot of the men who worked in her but who also served her masters well, steaming an estimated total of one million miles in her forty years.[51]

It would appear that rescue efforts failed and *St Margarets* left in February 1990 in tow with *Whimbrel* for the Naples area. She was probably lost en route but there are unconfirmed reports she was converted into a 'super yacht' or that there were at least plans for this (see photograph on p. 77).

Left: The *Ross Revenge* in 2014. *(C. O'Laoi)*

Below: The *Ross Revenge* arriving at Portsmouth with tug *George V*, 1980. *(Author's collection)*

Another historic and elegant cable ship acquired by Pounds was the *John W. Mackay*, completed in 1922 by Swan, Hunter & Wigham Richardson on the Tyne. Built for the Commercial Cable Company, in her early days she engaged on repair work on cables. After more than fifty years' service, she was laid up at Greenwich in 1977 where curiously she featured in a dramatic scene in the 1989 film *Indiana Jones and the Last Crusade*. Plans to preserve her as part of the Museum of London Docklands did not come to fruition and in 1990, she was acquired by Pounds and laid up on their buoys out in the harbour. Sadly, in February 1994, she was towed to Turkey for demolition as plans for her long-term preservation had come to nothing (see photographs on p. 78).

Former dockyard mooring lighter, *YC 484* (see p. 79) was the last steam-powered ship in the Royal Navy (although steam was only used for her ancillary boilers). She was sold for preservation to Belgian interests but sadly ended up being scrapped in the Netherlands.

The 1902 customs cutter *Vigilant* was given a berth by Pounds in the 1990s while preservation efforts were made (see photograph on p. 79). Following a period in the West Yard, she was last reported to be at Gillingham, in the hands of a charity associated with the Medway Maritime Trust.

Many other historic ships have passed through Pounds. Sometimes the background is unclear as with the purchase and quick resale of the celebrated 1900 schooner *Kathleen and May* in 1964. Besides *Demon*, several other nineteenth-century warships – once their active service life was over – became dockyard craft and then were bought by Pounds for further service around their yard.

MFV 119 'modernised' and converted to a holiday let, 2019.

MFV 119 in virtually her original
state, 1978. *(Peter Hales)*

St Margarets at Tipner. *(The News)*

Top: *John W. Mackay* awaiting the tow to the breakers' yard, February 1994. (*Jeremy Shaw*)
Above left: *John W. Mackay* was towed to the breakers by the tug *Soliman Reys*, February 1994. (*Jeremy Shaw*)
Above right: A sad sight – *John W. Mackay* at the breakers in Aliaga, Turkey. (*Selim San*)

YC 484 in the West Yard, early 1990s. *(Pounds)*

Vigilant in the West Yard, 2006. *(Ian Buxton)*

Lightships

Lightships had been occasionally bought in the past, but in July 1991 Pounds bought a batch of four that had become redundant for a reported £80,000. Lightships form a solid platform and are eye-catching, so it's unsurprising that three of them are still, over thirty years on, housing restaurants in Amsterdam, Rotterdam and Gosport, having been resold by Pounds. The fourth had a shorter and more unusual second life as a radio ship. More details appear in Appendix 2.

Left: Close-ups of three lightships at Tipner in September 1991.

Below: *Trinity Light Vessel 3* was sold by Pounds in 1995 for £30,000 for conversion to offshore radio ship *King David*. From 1996, she broadcast off the Israeli coast but sadly foundered in heavy gales in 2000. *(Mike Brand)*

P556 and other Submarines

Although the bow section and some other parts of *P556* were dismantled in 1982, she was to survive substantially intact in the East Yard at Tipner until around 1990 when her remnants were finally cut into sections to be shipped to Spain for melting down. *P556* therefore had a life span of nearly seventy years! Part of her fin lives on, preserved at Pounds' Fort Southwick as a memento.

Prior to *P556*, Pounds had bought and cut up six submarines after the First World War. Moreover, another historic link to submarines was that Tony Pounds-Cornish's father Bertram Cornish had served on the famous sub *E11* in the First World War. *E11* was a prolific hunter and sank over eighty ships.

During the 1980s, Pounds were to form a useful relationship with the RN Submarine Museum at Gosport, as George Malcolmson recalls:

The link between Pounds and the Museum revolved around Mr Harry Pounds [Young Harry] and wartime submariner Gus Britton [Ernest Charles Britton]. Gus would, if requested, provide some historical background for naval items that came into the yard. I suspect that in addition to general interest in the history [...] knowing historical significance would help establish intrinsic value.

I remember that Mr Harry Pounds once sent a car to collect Gus to bring him to the Pounds' home somewhere up near Bedhampton. I think it was for his birthday party. I know that the Museum also received first dibs on submarine-related items.

P556 at Tipner, *c.* 1973. Alongside is a Ton class minesweeper and in the distance the listing *Volage* can just be spotted. *(NMRN)*

Tony Pounds-Cornish 'on board' *P556, c.* 1973. *(The News)*

That link led to the transfer of the *Kaiten* submarine to the museum in 1986 (see photo on p. 84). Day to day, Malcolmson recalled Tony Pounds-Cornish was their main contact.

HMS *Statesman* was something of a one-off submarine purchase in 1961 and she would only be cut up in the early 1970s as part of the East Yard clearance. She had been active in the latter stages of the Second World War and is said to have fired more rounds from her gun than any other submarine during that conflict. In February 1945 off Sumatra, she forced four coasters to beach and sank an armed trawler. From 1951 to 1961, she served in the French Navy as *Sultane*.

Little was done with *Statesman* by Pounds after purchase, but in the early 1970s, contractor Sid Dean and his team broke her up, although they left intact the bronze fin.

Tiptoe and *Artemis* were bought in 1971 and 1972, for £32,000 and £23,844 respectively, by the normal competitive tender process. *Artemis* had unexpectedly sunk at her moorings at Gosport in 1971, trapping three men for ten hours, so it may be assumed that the lower price reflected her waterlogged condition. However, *Tiptoe* had been modernised, making her 1,410 tons as opposed to *Artemis* at 1,120 tons, explaining the higher price.

HMS *Statesman* in the East Yard, October 1966. Initial construction activity on the M275 can just be seen in the background. *(NMRN)*

Statesman with *VIC 33* (ex-*Smeaton*) to the left, and an unidentified MMS. *(NMRN)*

Fins of *P556* (right) and *Statesman*, 2005. Note the propeller and escape hatch lying on top of the fin of *P556*.

Sections of a rare Japanese *Kaiten* suicide submarine transferred from Pounds to the RN Submarine Museum, Gosport, and seen at its new home in 2002. It was moved to the Explosion Museum of Naval Firepower in 2011, where she remains in storage. The fin of the preserved *Alliance* can be seen in the background – her sister *Artemis* was demolished at Pounds.

HMS *Tiptoe* (left) and HMS *Artemis* on Pounds' moorings in November 1976. *(The late P.A. Vicary collection)*

Tiptoe being demolished. After being cut down, her hulk survived several years at Pounds. *Artemis* is just visible to the rear. *(Hill)*

Artemis in the course of final demolition, as was the large pontoon crane, in this dramatic 1994 view. *Pintail* can just be seen on the left of the photograph.

Main electrical motors from *Artemis*.

Remnants of *Artemis* at the break-up berth in 1994.

The hulk of *Tiptoe*, September 1989. Also in the background are sections of the hulls of *Bold Pathfinder* (left) and *P556*. *(Hinson)*

Two pictures above of the final days of *Tiptoe*. She is being finished off in these views taken in the East Yard in September 1991.

The O Class Submarine Project

Between 1992 and 1997, Pounds bought six Oberon class submarines in partnership with Leafield Logistics and Technical Services (see Table 3). Leafield had won a contract in 1992 against stiff competition to dispose of surplus Royal Navy material to friendly navies operating former RN craft. This was done on a profit-sharing basis with the MOD. Indeed, Leafield still, at the time of writing, have a significant role in this.

These diesel-powered submarines had been extremely successful in their operations with the Royal Navy. In all, thirteen were built for the Royal Navy and six were to end up at Tipner. Pounds were able to buy the six submarines at scrap prices (ranging for £43,000 to £69,000 each) but were mindful of the favourable prospects of selling spares from them to navies which still operated subs of that class. The hulks were then to be scrapped – this would not in itself have been profitable and sometimes the hulks were sold to third parties for break-up in situ at Tipner. Spares were sold usefully to the navies of Canada, Brazil and Chile. For example, *Orpheus* was stripped very quickly and her engines removed for the Chilean Navy subs *O'Brien* and *Hyatt*. *Orpheus* was then scrapped in 1995.

Table 3. Oberon Class Submarines Bought by Pounds, 1992–7

	Builder	Commissioned	Paid Off	Arrived at Pounds	Notes
Otter	Scotts, Greenock	20 Aug 1962	July 1991	March 1992	
Otus	Scotts, Greenock	5 Oct 1963	April 1991	1992	Resold June 2002 as museum ship
Orpheus	Vickers-Armstrongs, Barrow	25 Nov 1960	Sept 1987	1994	Had been harbour training ship after paying off
Opportune	Scotts, Greenock	29 Dec 1964	June 1993	1996	
Opossum	Cammell Laird, Birkenhead	5 June 1964	Aug 1993	Oct 1996	
Oracle	Cammell Laird, Birkenhead	14 Feb 1963	July 1993	1994	Left 31 October 2004 for break-up in Turkey.

Four *Oberon* class submarines laid up for disposal in Portsmouth harbour. *(R. Lindfield)*

Opportune in February 1997, cut down and flanked by former target ship *Bullseye* on the right. The latter became a houseboat at Hoo St Werburgh, then Grimsby, before being scrapped in 2006.

In a similar vein, in 1989 the Canadian government bought another submarine of the same class, *Osiris*, direct from the Royal Navy and cannibalised her at Birkenhead for spares for their own Oberon class submarines. In 1993 her hulk was broken up at Garston.

As an aside, Seaforth Maritime, a company unconnected to Pounds (and to the publisher of this book), bought *Oberon* and *Walrus* in 1986. These were similar subs to those Pounds acquired, and were purchased for an expensive total of £1.5m before being refurbished at Immingham. The intention was to sell them to foreign navies. The potential rewards were massive as *Olympus* had been sold to Canada in 1989 for £2.66m for training purposes; admittedly she was a 'warm' ship, just out of RN service. However, a sale for *Oberon* and *Walrus* did not materialise and they were scrapped at Grimsby from 1991.

Two of the submarines, *Otus* and *Oracle*, lingered on largely intact at Pounds for many years. Way back in 1992 there had been plans to open *Otus* as a restaurant in Torquay, but this never came about and so she remained at Pounds. *Otus* and *Oracle* attracted some local criticism as they rusted away. A local press article in October 2000, headlined 'Feelings run deep for silent warriors', hoped the subs would soon have a dignified end. There was even talk of local sculptor Alan Turner converting them into floodlit living sculptures supported on a concrete plinth and featuring water fountains:

> *A three-dimensional 'exploded' view of the submarine utilising the two halves of the hull, the deck casing and the two halves of the conning tower. The internal pressure hull will not be used. These elements of the submarine will be raised up and supported by a matrix of galvanised H girders which will be reminiscent of the structures used in shipbuilding. […] All piping, ducting and pumps necessary for the control and function of the pools of water and fountains will be visible and attached to the ceiling of the car park area. This is intended to echo the complex hydrodynamics of a submarine.*[52]

As it turned out, *Otus* was resold in June 2002 to be a museum ship at Sassnitz, a quiet resort town in the Baltic. Museum owner Carsten Nöhren-Petan had been scouring Europe for a suitable submarine. Pounds manager Dave McDermott was quoted as saying:

> *We were happy to get rid of her – and especially as she's not going to the breakers yard. There's nothing on her inside – she's stripped out and demilitarised, but you can still walk around, see how cramped she was and get an idea of the bunk space. It's nice to see her go and even nicer that she is not going to be scrapped but is going to be turned into a showpiece.*

After six weeks' renovation in dry dock at Stralsund, *Otus* was opened to the public at Sassnitz daily.[53] At the time of writing, in 2025, she is still a museum ship in Sassnitz, attracting 80,000 visitors each year.

Oracle was towed away in 2004 by a large German tug for break-up at Aliaga in Turkey. However, she did not reach her destination, foundering near Gibraltar and thus escaping the cutter's torch. Appendix 3 gives more details of the curious fate of *Oracle*.

Otus and *Orpheus*, July 1994. *(Steven Tacey)*

Above: Fin of *Orpheus* with fibreglass cladding, March 1995.

Above left: Escape hatch from *Orpheus*.

Left: *Otus* is towed away for a life in Germany as a museum ship by the tug *Taucher O. Wulf* No 5. (The News)

Otus and *Orpheus* in the West Yard, February 1994.

Otus and *Oracle* with the dredger *City of Bristol* in this view dating from August 1998.

Interior (probably *Orpheus*) opened up in July 1994. (*Steven Tacey*)

Films

The atmospheric Pounds yards at Portchester and Tipner, together with appropriate deployment of ships and other military debris, have on occasions made an excellent backdrop to well-known films, producing useful revenue for the Pounds business. The films are also of interest to the historian as they often will give a snapshot of the yard's appearance at a particular time.

The 1955 film *The Ship that Died of Shame* starred Geoge Baker and Richard Attenborough. It featured the wartime crew of a motor torpedo boat (MTB 1087) who find her in a scrapyard and buy her for clandestine operations. The scrapyard scenes were filmed at Pounds' Portchester yard and reveal a crowded but tidy facility with towering piles of scrap and long lines of Fairmile B motor launches moored offshore. Curiously, besides MTB 528 (presumably owned by Pounds), two other boats played 1087 in the film, namely fast patrol boat *Gay Dragoon* and a yacht *Taifun,* a Polish MTB. Coincidentally *Taifun* herself later sank while engaged in smuggling operations in the Mediterranean.

The 1958 film *The Key*, starring Trevor Howard and Sophia Loren, was set in the battle of the Atlantic in 1941. It was reputedly filmed at Pounds' Portchester yard, but largely in fact used Portland naval base. The film featured a Pounds ship, a torpedo recovery boat *Nettle* (acquired 1957), later renamed *Elfin.* Shortly after the filming, she was sold for further commercial service with the Amsterdam Dry Dock Company and became the last industrial steamship in the Netherlands. After retirement in 1989, she was rescued in 1995 by a group of enthusiasts and restored. Happily, she is very much still afloat as we go to press.

The 1968 film *Attack on the Iron Coast* was filmed in St Katharine's Dock in London's docklands. It featured a Pounds boat, a Ham class inshore minesweeper (second sub-group) in the starring role. The film's plot is based on the heroic Operation Chariot raid by British forces on St Nazaire in 1942. Tony Pounds-Cornish orchestrated operations of the various boats. Pounds received the useful sum of £1,864 for the use of their boats and associated costs from Mirisch Films.

Actors Richard Attenborough and George Baker stroll through the giant piles of scrap at Portchester. The giant tyres are perhaps from a Lancaster. *(Alamy)*

The most famous film featuring Pounds was *Tommy* (1975), which featured a number of rock stars including members of The Who (their lead singer Roger Daltrey starred) and Elton John. Most of the film was filmed in and around Portsmouth in 1974, including Pounds' Tipner yard. One classic scene features the cast playing pinball machines in the Pounds East Yard amongst old silver-painted marker floats, substantial

(*Alamy*)

MTB 528 (playing MTB 1087) as backdrop to actors Richard Attenborough (left) and George Baker. (*Alamy*)

(*Alamy*)

(*Alamy*)

Elfin featured in the 1958 film *The Key* and is seen here steaming in 2019. (*J. Plug*)

numbers of which were stacked up in the yard. An iconic song featured in the film is 'Pinball Wizard', and the silver-painted floats represent the pinballs. The star of the film, Roger Daltrey, then risks life and limb as he clambers up the silver floats to sing and initially at least direct operations (see image on p. 93). Harry Pounds himself was there to witness the filming and recalled the risks being taken. Towards the end of this section of the film, the camera turns briefly to a tank, its gun aimed crazily up to the sky.

The crowded state of the East Yard at that time is clear to see but the backdrop displays the almost rural location at the time of filming. As one bystander recalled:

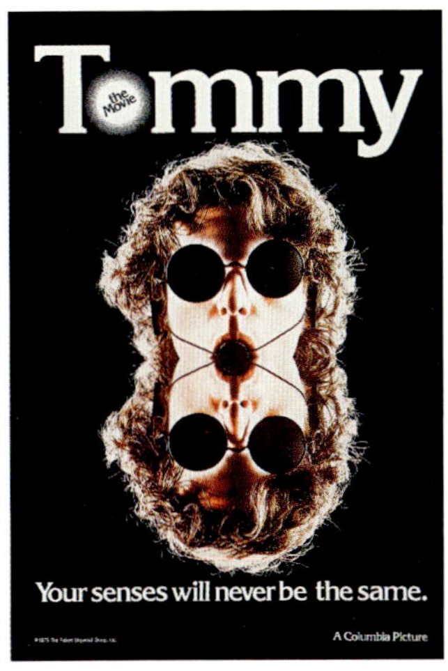

(Alamy)

Roger Daltrey standing on the silver pinballs/marker buoys, 1974. *(Alamy)*

Silver paint fading, the marker floats survive in this 1998 view.

I remember visiting the site when the M275 was being built and being amazed at the amount of metalwork on site. In particular, I remember some silver coloured spheres that I think had been used when Ken Russell made Tommy *in Portsmouth in 1974. As students, post 1st year exams, we got involved as extras in the film – a great experience. Especially being on the same stage at the same time as The Who and Elton John when the Pinball Wizard sequence was being filmed in Southsea. I even got to chat to Pete Townshend during another day's filming when I was a steward. Great fun.*

More film action soon followed at Pounds. The former Italian minesweepers *Arsella* and *Conchiglia* were bought by Pounds, apparently fit only for scrap (they were over twenty years old), however, they were to be adapted carefully for the 1978 film *The Greek Tycoon*, starring Anthony Quinn. For the film, loosely based on the life of shipping magnate Aristotle Onassis, the two minesweepers were fitted with a new replica Bofors gun armament and 'returned to naval service' renamed as the Norwegian patrol craft *Kvapp* and *Tana*. They were shrouded in artificial snow and filmed extensively in the Solent from the Pounds tug *Lord Ritchie*. Their glamorous new life as film extras was to last only a week or so and initial stripping and demolition commenced shortly thereafter. However, they were then laid up for two years prior to final break-up, one at Pounds and the other possibly at Sittingbourne.

Pounds also provided equipment for other films such as *Gladiator* (2000) and *Captain Corelli's Mandolin* (2001). They also supplied gear for two James Bond films, *Tomorrow Never Dies* (1997) and *The Spy Who Loved Me* (1977), as recalled in the local press:

> *Scrap from the yard was transformed for a scene with a ship and a submarine in Roger Moore's 1977 Bond film* The Spy Who Loved Me. *'For the latest film, the James Bond crew had engines from us and all sorts of gauges and panels to make up as a ship's engine room.' Pounds manager David McDermott said. Film publicist Geoff Freeman added, 'I can't say too much about what the engines were used for. They are part of a stealth ship which of course doesn't exist in real life, so we used our imagination – everything is sprayed silver. It plays a very important role in the film and on the stealth ship that the final confrontation takes place.'*[54]

Ships such as *Topmast 18* and military vehicles at Pounds have been used as an atmospheric backdrop to many pop and rock music videos.

The epic 1998 Steven Spielberg war film, *Saving Private Ryan*, begins with US forces landing on Omaha Beach in Normandy. Ten original wartime LCVPs – Landing Craft Vehicle / Personnel – were traced to desert storage in Palm Springs, California. Two British-built LCMs – Landing Craft Mechanised – were also located, and all twelve were restored to their 1944 appearance for filming at Wexford, Ireland. After the film two were snapped up by Pounds yard for potential resale.[55]

Pounds have, on occasion, allowed TV companies to film in the yard. The best example was in about 1994, when Toyah Willcox was filmed for BBC TV as she walked around the Pounds yard and into sheds. She talks to contractor Roger Allen and 'Marsh', a military historian, as they look around the yard at submarines, the three lightships, a Gnat aircraft and military vehicles including a Humber Pig and T-34 tank. Toyah refers to Pounds as being like a film set from *Raiders of the Lost Ark*. This fascinating 1994 film is well worth watching.[56]

In January 1987, the BBC1 programme *Tomorrow's World* featured presenter Peter Macann being filmed on board two submarines (probably *Artemis* and *P556*) at Pounds. He postulates about escaping if trapped inside any submarine and then proceeds to blow an explosive charge through the pressure hull of *P556*

Arsella and *Conchiglia* on arrival at the Camber, Portsmouth, in August 1976, to take part in filming of *The Greek Tycoon*. (Goss)

and crawl out. The resulting wave swamps the various other vessels present in the East Yard.

In 2004 an episode of the BBC TV series *Silent Witness*, 'Death by Water', was partly filmed at Pounds. Former landing ship tank (LST) *Stalker* was fitted with both dummy masts and radar and was renamed *Galle* for her new role. In the episode, Pounds was used as the 'Garner UK' yard and the storyline had poison gas seeping from the *Galle* causing illness among the local populace.

Stalker was the last surviving steam-powered LST in the world and had been acquired by Pounds in 2002, after becoming surplus to requirements at Rosyth. She had been a submarine support ship there for many years and previously served in this role at Derry/Londonderry. Built in Canada, she was completed slightly too late to see action in the war.

Pounds held off scrapping *Stalker* until 2010, while she was offered unsuccessfully to preservation groups. One charity even hoped to restore her to full working order. She was an LST (3) and could carry and land up to 170 troops and fifteen large tanks to shore. Her demolition was supervised by Lee Allen, son of Roger. Demolition concluded in 2012.

The hulk of *Arsella* (its film name *Tana* still evident). (Author's collection)

A Chieftain tank painted for a pop music video.

Filming for the Omaha Beach landings in *Saving Private Ryan* cost US$12m over a four-week period and involved 1,500 actors. *(Alamy)*

This 1998 view shows *PA30-10*, far from the Normandy beaches, in the West Yard at Pounds. *Demon* and a crane pontoon just are visible to right, as is the floating footbridge formerly in No 3 basin of Portsmouth Dockyard.

The 'other' Pounds landing craft, now fully restored and exhibited at Le Grand Bunker, Ouistreham, Normandy. (*Le Grand Bunker*)

An evocative image of Omaha landing craft from the film *Saving Private Ryan*. (Alamy)

LST *Stalker* rechristened *Galle* for BBC TV's *Silent Witness*.

Military Vehicles

The focus of this book has been on Pounds' substantial and varied shipping activities. However general dealing in other scrap, equipment and reusables has probably been the major element of the business throughout. Pounds often bought military surplus from the War Office,[57] or at auction sales, mainly around the UK. These might occur when an establishment such as the Woolwich Arsenal was closing, for example, and competitive prices might be obtained as the War Office or other vendors were looking to clear the site in question.

Pounds have purchased military vehicles in huge quantities, running into hundreds or quite possibly thousands. Normally bought for break-up for scrap, these comprised nearly all steel, although some more valuable non-ferrous metals, typically copper and bronze, were recovered. Periscopes have a low market value but, in some cases, ended up being sold to collectors and museums, as would also of course complete tanks or other vehicles.

Pounds was one of several breakers which took surplus military vehicles, and it has been reported occasionally that they were the largest such enterprise in the UK. Evidence for this is scarce but their operations were clearly substantial.

Pounds often retained an example of each vehicle type. On a visit by the author to Pounds in September 1991, it was noted, for example, that there was one Bren gun carrier, Churchill, T-34, Sherman, one Centaur converted as a bulldozer and another as a Churchill Armoured Recovery Vehicle (ARV) and a Stuart converted Gun Tractor. There was also an Army AEC Armoured Command Vehicle rumoured to have been used by 'Monty', Field Marshal Montgomery, 1st Viscount Montgomery of Alamein. This is currently being restored in Kent.

At Pounds, there would often be a delay before most military vehicles were broken up, which is unusual for the scrap business. This resulted in piles of vehicles, particularly in the East Yard, and by the 1970s, this had become something of a jungle as vegetation took over. This yard was gradually cleared in the 1970s and 1980s.

Rare examples or types might be resold on occasions or, sometimes, would be donated to collectors or museums. The Sherman Beach Armoured Recovery Vehicle (BARV), pictured on p. 102, is now on display at the D-Day Experience

Bren gun carrier (*T16*), also known as the Universal Carrier. Built by Ford in the United States, it has a post-war registration number painted on the side.

A rare AEC (Associated Equipment Company) armoured command vehicle (ACV), reputedly used by Monty.

A rare Churchill Mk 2 ARV fitted with fake turret and gun to fool the enemy.

A Centaur Dozer tank. This vehicle has had a remarkable history, being built originally by Leyland Motors in 1944 as an A27L (Liberty engined) Centaur tank. In 1944 she had lost her turret when converted to a bulldozer. Discovered at Pounds by a collector, she underwent a near fifteen-year restoration, which was concluded in 2016.

Museum in Portsmouth. It is a modified Sherman tank, originally built in the USA in 1943. Its function was to push landing craft back out to sea and clear other vehicles that had got stuck or damaged on the beaches. This particular vehicle probably served on the Normandy beaches in 1944. After purchase by Pounds after the war ended, it was one of three similar vehicles that were used to drag other vehicles around the Pounds yard.

A Stuart Gun Tractor (converted from an M5A1 Stuart Tank) and, behind, an M10 tank destroyer and a M51 Sherman Tank. The latter was originally US built, then likely deployed by the French Army and later was definitely used by the Israel Defense Forces and the Lebanese Army.

A Sexton 25pdr self-propelled gun. This was a Canadian-designed vehicle from the Second World War, of which 2,150 were built. It remained in service until 1956.

Also at the D-Day Experience is a Churchill Crocodile Mark VII flame thrower tank, now displayed on board the restored Landing Craft Tank (LCT) *7074*. The museum acquired the BARV and the Crocodile in 1986 and 1988 respectively from Pounds, and they were then restored by the Military Vehicle Trust.

Other museums have been fortunate to acquire historic tanks from Pounds. For example, the Museum of the Battle of Normandy at Bayeux, France, has a M4A1 Sherman tank (pictured on p. 102).

Bulk purchases of military vehicles were made. In August 1962, for example, £3,790 was paid to the War Office for 'armoured cars'. Single tanks

BARV, ex-Pounds, about to be refurbished in a 2002 view. *(D-Day Experience)*

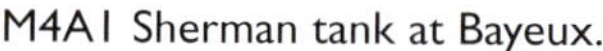

M4A1 Sherman tank at Bayeux.

or vehicles were sold for as little as £9 to enthusiasts, no doubt with the buyer having to arrange and pay for collection and delivery. As Tony Pounds-Cornish recalled:

> *In the 50s you could not give a tank away. The war was too recent in people's minds. Now the younger generation is interested and buys vehicles to restore them. Some end up better than new.*

Purchases were made not only in the UK but also around the world as military activity reduced at various locations. Tanks might be bought and cut up in situ rather than incurring the heavy costs and trouble of bringing them to the Pounds yard. An example of this occurred in 1958, when an assignment for Pounds to cut up 183 tanks took place at the former US base at Sealand in Flintshire, Wales.

Toyah, in her 1994 TV report, featured several military vehicles including a Humber FV1611 'Pig' Armoured Personnel Carrier (APC) (see p. 103) and a T-34 Russian tank.[58]

Maybe a book will be written on Pounds and military vehicles one day.

Humber FV1611 Pig armoured personnel carrier, seen here in September 1991. A lightly armoured truck, this became well known on the streets of Northern Ireland during the Troubles.

An ex-Canadian Ford Carrier Windsor Mk 1*. Also on view are two Centaur Dozer Tanks (one below the Windsor and one to the right). *(After the Battle magazine)*

However, in 1982, *After the Battle* magazine described the treasure trove of military hardware at Pounds, based on an earlier (1978) visit made to the yard by editor Winston Ramsey:

In the years following the ending of the Second World War, scrap metal was in great demand as European industry geared itself for the conversion to peace, the mass production era, and the replacement of its ageing machinery. Allied armour, no longer of use to the armed forces, began arriving in the form of Covenanters, Cromwells, Achilles, Sextons, and Priests, to be followed later by the Churchill and Stuart. Shermans never featured in the post war scrap sales as they still found ready markets with many overseas armies. Most of the vehicles were 'non runners' and after being offloaded from their transporters at Pounds, tanks would be towed piggyback fashion on top of others in an effort to cram in as much as possible. Others would be craned into position forming incredible piles forty and fifty feet high [...] soft-skinned vehicles – jeeps, GMCs, Whites, Macks and Champs also arrived at the yard, but the WWII armour really finished coming around 1953/6. Although 90% was cut up and delivered to smelters

Self-propelled mounting for a 25pdr Sexton II of Canadian origin with a postwar British registration number. This vehicle was returned to Canada in 1981 for restoration by the Canadian Military Heritage Society in Rockwood, Ontario. A Churchill Mk VII Crocodile can be seen on the left. (After the Battle *magazine*)

– probably ending in today's motorcars – the bottom dropped out of the scrap market in the mid-1960s. From that time onward the price paid for scrap at the mills was less than the cost of cutting it up and hence most vehicles already in the yard were stockpiled against better days in the future. Fortunately for enthusiasts, although not necessarily for Pounds, the situation still prevails today, resulting in the forced preservation of many tanks, carriers and the like. As Henry Pounds is keen to retain one of each vehicle as a representative sample of those, which have passed through the yard, several interesting museum pieces are not for sale, including a Beach Armoured Recovery Vehicle (also used to tow or rather drag vehicles around in the yard). Most of what is left today is either engineless, difficult if not impossible to extract, or in bad condition.

Over the last five years, the removal of armour and the salvaging of other equipment and the construction of new concrete roads have transformed the scrapyard. Vast quantities of military equipment still remain to be seen although the 'graphic architecture of war's debris' is no longer apparent in 1982. The intrusion of British Rail diesel cabs and the like marks the passing of time as a new generation's scrap replaces the old. We can only guess what secrets still remain beneath the piles of metal, which mark probably the last armoured graveyard in the UK.[59]

Tanks were only rarely purchased after the death of Old Harry in 1971. After he passed away, contractor Sid Dean estimates that he demolished about fifty

A Churchill MK VII Crocodile flamethrower infantry tank awaits its fate. (After the Battle *magazine*)

tanks and fifty Bren gun carriers in the early 1970s as part of his clearance of the East Yard.

In early 1993 Pounds bought twenty-two Chieftain tanks from the MOD. Tony Pounds-Cornish is pictured with some of them (see p. 106), all lined up in the East Yard, having arrived on a low loader from Wiltshire. Commenting on their selling price Tony recalled:

Anyone interested would be pleasantly surprised. They're all perfectly maintained and sealed against the elements. The only thing that doesn't work is the guns, they've been decommissioned.[60]

After three months, nine of the twenty-two had been sold, the top price achieved having been £7,500.

The remains of military vehicles were gradually cleared from the yard with some of the last ones being sold for display at the Hop Farm at Beltring in Kent. Scattered around the yard for many years were remnants, including two former German 105mm guns used in their abortive siege of Stalingrad and then captured by the Russians and re-barrelled for use in their onslaught on Berlin. These are now on display at Fort Southwick.

Well before the closure of the Pounds business in 2023, all the tanks and military vehicles had been cleared away, mainly sold or donated to collectors and museums. A few have been the subject of careful restoration and are stored at Fort Southwick.

On the left in this photograph is a Dodge T245 ¾ ton 4×4 M43 ambulance, ex-US Army Medical Force, c. 1950. This and three previous 1978 images taken from the article 'Portsmouth Graveyard', by Winston Ramsey. (After the Battle *magazine*)

These Churchill Mark VII Crocodile flamethrower tanks, seen in 1983, had quite possibly have been at Pounds since the late 1950s. (*R. Stickland*)

Tony Pounds-Cornish with a line of Chieftain tanks acquired 1993. Military buffs may notice that the second tank back in the photo is painted in the 'Berlin urban camouflage' scheme, favoured sometimes over the country green in case the Soviets invaded and battles took place on the streets of Berlin. The design is somewhat akin to the dazzle camouflage sometimes deployed by the Royal Navy during the First World War. (*The News*)

A closer view of the Chieftain Mk 10 Main Battle Tank from the Berlin Brigade. *(R. Stickland)*

Two ex-US Army LARC-LXs, nos 16 and 50, which had 60-ton cargo capacity, were bought jointly with Ross Veitch of A.F. Ross and Sons in the 1990s. After years of vandalism, one was demolished but there is a possibility that the other was preserved at a US museum, although it was probably also broken up.

A crowded scene in 1994 with a former runway control unit on the left and three Bandvagn Bv 202s made by Bolinder-Munktell in Sweden. The Bvs were small snow vehicles used in Arctic regions.

A Mowag Training Tank made in Switzerland, an example of a vehicle restored and displayed at Fort Southwick by Pounds.

Aeroplanes and Trains

Planes were occasionally purchased, presumably for resale as static items to enthusiasts after maybe a good purchasing opportunity arose.

Purchases of locomotives for scrap were often made by shipbreakers, particularly in the 1960s, when the use of rail steam engines was being phased out. There is little obvious evidence of this activity with Pounds although occasional purchases were made, for example, £8,840 paid in December 1966 to the British Railways Board for 'scrap engines' and Winston Ramsey refers to the arrival of diesel cabs in the 1970s in the extract from his article on pp. 103–104. Evidence suggests that locomotives were broken up at Fratton and Eastleigh on the other side of Portsmouth as no railway lines came into or close to Pounds' yards at Portchester or Tipner. Clearance work of locos and track was possibly done also by Pounds at the Longmoor military railway when it closed in 1969.

A former RAF Avro Anson. In September 1988, it was reported that a key panel from the cockpit had sadly been stolen, presumably to order. *(Pounds)*

A Hawker Hunter in 1995. Now preserved at the former RNAS Ford, this plane (GA11, serial no WW654) had been a member of the RN Blue Herons, which in 1976 was the world's first jet aerobatic team.

Two Gnats as used by the Red Arrows. One (T.1 XM694) was sold to Everett Aero in Ipswich in 1995.

CHAPTER 6

THE FINAL DAYS AND CLOSURE IN 2023

Stalker (see pp. 95, 98) was the last major ship to be broken up at Pounds, her demolition being concluded in 2012. The scrap market for ships has become more difficult, with the Royal Navy almost invariably selling to breakers at Aliaga in Turkey for break-up; wage costs are lower there and operations are streamlined and conducted near to steel mills.

From the early days at Portchester, cranes have been bought and scrapped or sold on by Pounds. Two large floating cranes were acquired by Pounds in the final years; the taller one, *Canute*, dominated the Portsmouth skyline, having arrived from Southampton Docks in 2015. The pontoon and possibly the *Canute* crane were built in 1970 for Associated British Ports by Wilton-Fijenoord. A smaller *Apache* crane is ex-US Army and possibly dates from the 1940s. It was hired out to third parties and also lifted smaller vessels onshore for breaking, as is best practice now. Harry Pounds (son of Young Harry) and his team continued to trade in ships and break some up. The ships tended to be small, ranging from tugs to coasters although unusual purchases were sometimes made. For example, in 2018, the substantial Continental Ferry Port linkspan from Portsmouth was bought and was scrapped by contractors in 2021.

The far end of the West Yard was leased to Breedon (previously Lafarge were tenants) who used the deep-water berths for shipments of sand, gravel and ready-mix concrete. In later years, this far end became vacant and was used by Pounds for storage.

Other parts of the West Yard were sublet to third parties including a waste disposal firm using the industrial unit. The East Yard was cleared at an earlier stage, in anticipation of development for housing.

Fort Southwick was acquired by the Pounds family in around 2003. Built in the 1860s, it is a massive brick structure on Portsdown Hill overlooking Portsmouth harbour. Acquired as a property investment, it also houses, in part,

The dredger *Donald Redford* (left), leaving the leased end of the West Yard with a cargo of aggregate passing *Brinton* in 2002.

a collection of relics from the business's activities, including military vehicles and parts of ships – for example, the fins of both *P556* and *Statesman*. Fort Southwick is now something of a museum to the family's endeavours in this most successful and fascinating business.

Over the years there have been many reports of the whole Tipner area being redeveloped. Plans have been thwarted by access problems from the M275, now resolved to a significant extent by a park and ride facility requiring a new exit from the motorway. Also, Tipner lake, adjacent to the East Yard, has now been designated as a site of special scientific interest. The whole area has seen a wide range of heavy industry in the last two centuries, including chemical plants and brickworks, meaning the soil is somewhat contaminated, as is the case with many comparable sites.

These difficulties seem to have been overcome. As we go to press, it is reported that the West Yard has possibly been sold for redevelopment to the local council. This has required Harry Pounds to arrange for clearing of the entire site prior to completion of the sale. So, the present site will be transformed for modern housing and shopping units – a less alluring sight perhaps for visitors driving into Portsmouth than the view at present.

A general view of the West Yard in February 2020. Seen here are the two cranes, *Apache* (left) and *Canute*. On the right is the hull of one of the Girl tugs, *Susan*, and on the left on the quayside can be seen her superstructure. She was in the middle of a conversion to a houseboat that was never finished. On the left are the tugs *Nancy*, inboard of *Joan*. On the extreme right, outboard, is *Hamnfjord*. (Stephen Wenham)

Former ferry port linkspan, May 2020.
(*Stephen Wenham*)

The restored fin of HMS *Statesman*
preserved at Fort Southwick.

Hamnfjord (1905/140) was to be the last ship to be broken up at Pounds. Originally a fishing vessel, it is reported that she became a cargo ship post-1945. *(Stephen Wenham)*

The ex-RMAS tugs, *Joan* and *Nancy*, had been at Tipner for seven years when pictured in May 2020 with the former Hayling Island ferry pontoon. *(Stephen Wenham)*

The 1925 Humber barge *Hen*, converted into a houseboat at Pounds. *(Theobald-Moulds)*

Fort Southwick.

The West and East Yards largely cleared except for the *Canute* crane, October 2022. *(S. Chalk)*

CHAPTER 7

AERIAL VIEWS OF THE HARRY POUNDS YARDS

A splendid view of the whole Tipner site in late 1981 or early 1982. In the West Yard (foreground), on this side of the motorway, can be seen *Admiralty Floating Dock 21* and inboard of her, *Topmast 18*. Moving away from the M275 is the black-hulled customs vessel *Vigilant*. Down from the floating crane is the submarine *Artemis* and round the corner is *Coast Farmer*, then the three ships to her right are *Demon* (by shore), *Whimbrel* and *Pirelle*. In the more distant East Yard, *Howitzer* is to the top of the image, two subs *P556* and *Tiptoe*, while *Volage* is hardly visible alongside the Mulberry Harbour. Further down is the 'horned' LCF *34* with the black-hulled *Isis* close by. (*University of Portsmouth*)

A July 1983 view showing the East Yard (foreground) and beyond the motorway is the West Yard. Most of the ships present are also in the image on p. 114, but *AFD 21* has gone, as has *Isis*. *(Portsmouth City Museums)*

Military vehicles abound in this shot of East Yard in 1972 or early 1973; the M275 has not yet been opened. From the right are the two Ton class minesweepers *Fiskerton* and *Leverton*, the 'horned' LCF *34*, submarines *P556* and *Statesman*, *Bold Pathfinder* alongside *Broadley*, and, on the extreme left is *Puncheston*. *(City Secretariat Portsmouth)*

East Yard, 21 July 1983. Moving round the shore from the right, discernible vessels are LCF *34*, the stern of *P556*, 'sternless' frigate *Volage* and submarine HMS *Tiptoe*. Further round are the bows of a Ton class minesweeper perhaps *Repton*, LCI (S) *Kingfisher*, then an apparently intact *Bold Pathfinder* and finally what appears to be a *TID* tug. *(University of Portsmouth)*

East Yard, late 1987. Most of the military vehicles have been cleared, but from left to right can be seen *Shipham* and what are believed to be the hulks of two steam-driven tugs. Then, just visible, is the square end of Fairmile LCI (S) *Kingfisher* and submarines *Tiptoe* and *P556* – both would be gone within four years. Between the two subs is the cut-down hulk of the frigate *Volage*. To the right is the rare Second World War-era LCF *34*. Various other hulks of uncertain vintage are half-sunk or buried – the one on extreme right is probably the First World War *Eivis*. *(University of Portsmouth)*

The West Yard in July 1990. Just above the floating crane can be seen two Ham class minesweepers *Shipham* and *Fordham*. Alongside submarine *Artemis* are *Thorngarth*, *Waterwitch* and former customs vessel *Vigilant*. Round the corner are *Pintail* and *Demon*. *(University of Portsmouth)*

The West Yard, probably mid-1992. Top right is the ferry *Brading* and further right the submarine *Otter*. Moving to the left we see three of the four lightships bought in the summer of 1991 and the three US *ST* tugs. Inboard of *Pintail* can just be made out the cut-down hull of the submarine *Artemis*. Outboard of the pontoon crane are *Shipham*, *Fordham* and *Vigilant*, and to its left the fleet tender *Manly*. Onshore, further to the left, can be seen the two 4.5-inch gun turrets. *(K. Didwell)*

APPENDIX 1

BUSINESS ENTITIES

This book refers throughout to the Harry Pounds business and to the reader of this book and the outside world, that was really all that mattered in the normal course of events. However, it is interesting to note briefly who and what owned and operated the Pounds business.

As far as can be discerned, Frederick Pounds operated as a sole trader in his own name, as did his son H.G. Pounds (Old Harry), from when he started until the 1960s (see the letterhead illustration below). In 1961 Old Harry and the Pounds business started trading through a limited company, Pounds Shipowners and Shipbreakers Ltd (PSSB). This was controlled by Old Harry with his wife. His son Young Harry had a one-third share.

The business entity Paulsgrove Salvage and Shipbreaking Co Ltd is noted as trading in 1954 (it acquired an LCT) but its history and use is uncertain. The diver's helmet image on its notepaper and the word 'salvage' in the name suggests an activity of which the author has little or no information. The company was dissolved at least twenty-five years ago (see letterhead below).

Pounds Marine Shipping Ltd was formed in 1970 and was controlled by Young Harry. From around this time, it formed, with PSSB, the main trading companies.

Two special-purpose vehicles have been in existence:

- Cairnryan Port Company Ltd was formed to acquire Cairnryan in 1960.
- Trafalgar Wharves Ltd was formed in 1965 to hold the West Yard property at Tipner.

All companies have been owned by members of the Pounds family only; there were no outside shareholders.

Accounts for the limited companies are available on the public record at Companies House for nearly all years, but often only in abbreviated form, as this is all that is required by law.

For some other years, figures can be estimated from accounting records. For example, in 1961 when Old Harry and PSSB were trading, third-party sales were £314,000 and payments £300,000, giving a profit of £14,000. This does not sound much, but in present monetary terms this would be a profit of up to £300,000. This figure of £14,000 must be treated with caution, however, as it is based on cash receipts and payments, thus stocks and amounts owed and owing are not considered.

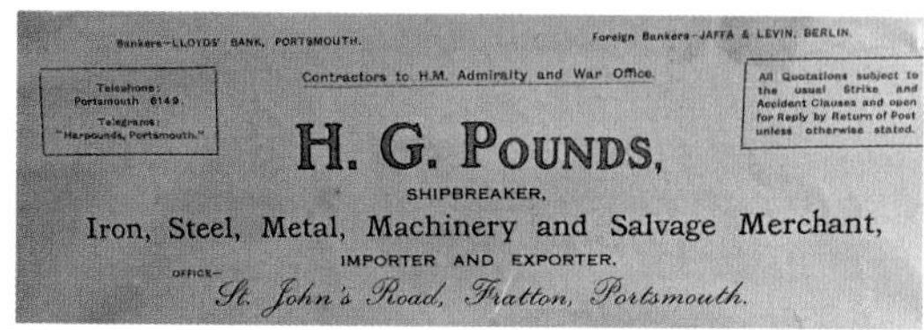

LIST OF SHIPS BOUGHT BY HARRY POUNDS' BUSINESSES, 1921–2023

The Bibliography and Sources section on pp. 142–3 sets out in detail the various sources used in compiling this list.

Notes on ship list:

1. Despite valuable help from the Pounds family and maritime historians with considerable knowledge of Pounds, it is not always clear whether a ship, once acquired, was sold on for further service or broken up. Appropriate comments may be found in the notes on available data.
2. A ship may be seen on Pounds moorings, but it is not always clear whether Pounds acquired her.
3. The 'bought' column in the list is a best estimate, where known. It may be date of arrival or date first seen at the yard, date of payment for ship, for example. It is likely that a number of ships have been omitted from the list and readers' information or views are always most welcome.
4. Abbreviations:
   Bt   bought
   Bu   broken up
   Lu   laid up

Page references in italic refer to ships in photographs and referred to in captions.

Name	Type	Built	GRT	Displnt	Bought	Cost (£)	Text ref
D4	submarine	1911	–	550	19.12.21	775	–
D4, D7 and D8 below were removed from Portsmouth dockyard 16.2.22 and Bu Fareham.							
D7	submarine	1911	–	550	19.12.21	775	–
D8	submarine	1911	–	550	19.12.21	775	–
UC-95	German submarine	1918	–	571	1922	–	–
UC-95 and the two other U-boats below reported to have been Bu at Fareham.							
U-67	German submarine	1915	–	933	1922	–	–
UB-64	German submarine	1917	–	508	1922	–	–
Swordfish	submarine	1916		932	17.7.22	2,007	–
Experimental steam turbine submarine, resold to Hayes Porthcawl, Wales, 1923 for Bu.							
No 76	tug	–	–	–	3.23	110	–
Bt for £110 with Mistletoe.							
Mistletoe	tug	1897	–	30	3.23	–	–
Ex-Laurel. Resold to Sharpness New Docks, 1923.							
Fresco	tug	1915	–	74	1923	1,350	–
Resold for commercial use and later Bu Bo'ness 1963.							
Excelsior	ex-fishing vessel	–	–	–	1924	780	–
Sank off Isle of Wight 6.9.24 while carrying scrap iron cargo to Newport, Monmouthshire.							
Vernon I	torpedo school	1859	–	5,481	16.5.25	3,707	12, 13, 14, 15
Ex-sailing battleship Donegal, see text for full story.							
Insolent	gate vessel	1881	–	265	24.6.25	101	9
Former iron screw gunboat, became gate vessel 1918 and then foundered 1.7.22 in Fountain Lake.							
A2	submarine	1902	–	190	27.10.25	101	8, 9
Had been wreck in Bomb Ketch Lake, Fareham. Bt by 'Old Harry' Pounds.							
YC I	mooring lighter	–	–	–	17.6.26	200	23
Bt by 'Old Harry' Pounds at Portland auction. 80-ft wooden dumb mooring lighter.							
Mystery	wood lighter	–	–	200	17.6.26	200	–
Bt by F.W. Pounds at Torpoint auction.							
YC 302	yard craft	–	–	–	5.5.27	500	–
Ex-John Penn.							
YC 16	yard craft	–	–	–	28.6.27	175	–
Bt at Sheerness auction.							
Carrigaline	tug, ex-WO mining launch	1892	21	–	26.8.27	–	–
Possibly used as yard tug, Bu 1930.							
V44	ex-German DD	–	–	–	1927	–	9
Both V44 and V82 (below) Bt from T.W. Ward, shipbreakers, see text for full story.							
V82	ex-German DD	–	–	–	1927	–	8, 9
YC 86	yard craft	–	–	–	27.6.1928	144	23
Bt at Sheerness.							
YC 3	yard craft	–	–	–	28.6.1928	310	–
Princess	tug/fire float	1903	78	–	10.28	–	–
I	steam lighter	1886	72	–	1928	–	–
Renamed Harpounds. Resold 1936 for further service.							
Treffry	tug	1870	46.	–	2.1933	–	–
Bt from Edward Treffry, sold 1934 to McMenemy, Woolwich.							
Hopper No 8	hopper	1905	51	–	9.6.1933	250	–
Bt from Great Western Railway. Paperwork in TNA Kew, file RAIL 252/2243. Resold and Bu Passage West 1981.							
Treffry	tug	1870	46	–	1934	–	–
Bt back (see above). Resold Woolcock, Havant, 1934, wrecked Dunkirk 6.34.							
X 41	barge	–	–	–	1936	–	–
Sold to a Mr J.J. Chalmers.							
Rosslea	flat	1904	105	–	1936	–	–
Cameron	steamship	1919	1,190	–	1940	–	–
Marmion	passenger ship	1906	409	–	1941	–	15
A wreck at Harwich, following air attack. A minesweeper in both world wars.							
Beaulieu	tug	1901	58	–	10.1.43	–	–
Resold 19.5.45 to White, Cowes.							
LCI 254	LCI(L)	–	–	–	1943	–	16
Likely many similar craft to this and the next two would have been bought.							
LCI 314	LCI(L)	–	–	–	1943	–	–
LCT 868	LCT (4)	–	–	–	1944	–	17
Beaulieu	tug	1901	58	–	30.12.45	–	–
Bt back, resold 1948 to Voke and Goad, Newhaven. Bu 1950.							

Name	Type	Built	GRT	Displnt	Bought	Cost (£)	Text ref
Lupin	accommodation hulk, ex-sloop	1916	–	1,250	22.3.46	–	–
Refloated and Bu by Pounds.							
Carbon	tug	1896	185	–	7.9.46	–	–
Ex-*John Holloway*. Sank off Isle of Wight before arrival Portchester.							
P556	submarine	1922	–	640	24.1.47	–	15, 16, 17 18, 81, 82, 84, 116
See text for full story and images.							
Sea Mule 1670	sea mule	1940s	37	–	19.2.47		–
Sea mules were small tugs and over 8,000 were built by Chrysler during the Second World War. Boxy and functional. Of those bought by Pounds, an unknown number were sold to Anglo-Eastern Trading 3.6.47 for £2,000.							
Sea Mule 1656	sea mule	1940s	37	–	19.2.47	–	–
Sea Mule 1637	sea mule	1940s	37	–	19.2.47	–	22
Sea Mule 1667	sea mule	1940s	37	–	19.2.47	–	–
Sea Mule 111	sea mule	1940s	37	–	19.2.47	–	–
Sea Mule 1956	sea mule	1940s	37	–	19.2.47	–	–
Sea Mule 1965	sea mule	1940s	37	–	19.2.47	–	–
Sea Mule 592	seal mule	1940s	37	–	19.2.47	–	–
Sea Mule 629	sea mule	1940s	37	–	19.2.47	–	–
Sea Mule 1664	sea mule	1940s	37	–	13.5.47	–	–
Sea Mule 1666	sea mule	1940s	37	–	13.5.47	–	–
Sea Mule 1103	sea mule	1940s	37	–	13.5.47	–	–
Sea Mule 1668	sea mule	1940s	37	–	13.5.47	–	–
Sea Mule 1969	sea mule	1940s	37	–	13.5.47	–	–
Sea Mule 1978	sea mule	1940s	37	–	13.5.47	–	–
VIC 10	stores carrier	1942	96	–	23.8.47	–	–
Resold 1949 for commercial service in the Netherlands and then Norway.							
Éclair	tug	–	59	–	29.11.47	–	91, 92
Resold to Percival Biddlecombe, Southampton, 3 1950 and Bu.							
MTB 528	motor torpedo boat	1946	–	480	1.3.48	–	–
Featured in the 1955 film *The Ship that Died of Shame*, which was filmed in part at Pounds yard, Portchester.							
Sea Mule 1676	sea mule	1940s	37	–	28.5.48	–	–
Flamer	dockyard tug	1915	124	–	1.6.48	–	–
Ex-*C108, YC298*.							
St Mellons	naval tug	1918	860	–	9.8.48	–	–
Bu by Pounds.							
C154b	coal lighter	–	–	–	8.10.48	–	–
Solent	paddle ferry	1902	161	–	1948	–	19, 20
Bu *c.* 1957.							
F.W. No 23	tug	1900	97	–	1948	–	–
Bt from Frazer White (FW) and resold 1949 to James Contracting for further service.							
Foxhound	tug	1903	92	–	1.49	–	–
Ex-*Blazer*. Bt from Bristol Channel Towage, lingered at Tipner until at least the late 1960s.							
Adolf Kuhling	tug	–	–	–	6.12.49	–	–
War prize, ex-German ship passed to Pounds by Ministry of Transport.							
Gilgenburg	German tug	1943	532	–	1949	–	–
Resold 1950 to Norwegian interests and converted to sealer. Foundered 1975.							
Hugo Heincke	German tug	1941	532	–	1949	–	–
Resold 1950 to Norwegian interests and converted to sealer. Foundered 1973.							
Schwalbenberg	German tug	1943	532	–	1949	–	–
Resold 1954 to Pakistani interests as *Moeen*.							
Medway	unknown	1893	–	–	1949	–	–
Collingwood	trawler	1902	179	–	1949	–	–
X 95	X lighter	1915	130	–	31.7.50	–	–
X 149	X lighter	1915	130	–	23.1.51	–	–
VWL 12	water lighter	1946	136	–	13.10.51	920	–
Ex-*MOB 9*, resold Everard as *Attunity* for further service.							
VWL 11	water lighter	1945	136	–	13.12 51	920	–
Ex-*MOB 8*, resold Everard as *Apexity* for further service.							
C158	oil fuel lighter	1905	400	–	1951	–	50, 51
See text for more detail.							
Florence	tug?	1900	139	–	1951	–	–

Name	Type	Built	GRT	Displnt	Bought	Cost (£)	Text ref
VIC 49	stores lighter	1944	147		22.9.52	–	–
Resold for further commercial service in Norway 1953. Reported Bu 2007.							
X134	cable lighter	1915	172	–	1952	–	22
Seen at Portchester around 1954 during filming of *The Ship that Died of Shame*.							
RCL 907	RCL	–	–	–	5.10.53	–	–
902	unknown	–	–	–	5.10.53	–	–
C914	RCL	–	–	–	14.10.53	–	–
C915	RCL	–	–	–	14.10.53	–	–
NAVI	steel lighter	–	–	–	27.10.53	–	–
C9 (a)	coal hulk	1809	–	–	30.12.53	–	–
Ex-HMS *Ajax*, had become coal hulk in 1860.							
C11a	coal lighter	1932	–	–	30.12.53	–	–
Sold to British Rail 1954 who used her as a coal hulk for their ferries.							
C31b	lighter	1904	50	–	30.12.53	–	–
Alternative name *C11*							
C29b	fuel lighter	1938	–	–	30.12.53	–	–
Resold for private use. Bu *c.* 1988.							
Malta	launch	1946	–	–	9.2.54	–	–
Resold for private use. Bu *c.* 1988.							
Mandora	launch	1946	–	–	9.2.54	–	–
The above two were RASC general service ('Barrack Lines' class) launches.							
RCL112	cargo lighter	–	–	–	4.8.54	–	–
C129	tug	1940	46	–	1955	–	–
Resold to Harry Rose (Towage), Poole as *Wendy Ann 3*.							
Freija	salvage vessel	–	–	–	19.1.55	–	29
Resold after 1958 for further service.							
NA 1	armament lighter	–	–	–	17.10.55	576	49
MMS 1606	motor minesweeper	1942	–	225	12.1.56	–	–
Valiant	pontoon lighter – hulk	–	–	–	10.5.56	–	–
MMS 1801	motor minesweeper	1943	–	225	20.8.56	–	–
MMS 1609	motor minesweeper	1942	–	225	8.56	–	–
Sir Robert Whigham	target towing vessel	1931	–	152	8.12.56	2,750	–
MMS 1685	motor minesweeper	1942	–	225	1956	–	21
Resold 20.11.56.							
MMS 1803	motor minesweeper	1942	–	225	1956	–	–
Resold 8.56							
MMS 1077	motor minesweeper	1944	–	369	1956	–	–
Resold 20.7.56							
Hollybranch	cargo ship	1917	301	–	1956	–	–
Resold to the Netherlands and Bu 1956.							
Urgent	water tank vessel	1910	224	–	1956	3,500	–
VIC 24	stores lighter	1942	96	–	23.1.57	–	–
Resold for further commercial service as *Advance*.							
MOB 7	tanker	1945	136	–	20.2.57	–	–
Bt from RASC, then resold 15.4.57 for Everard as *Tankity*. Bu 1968.							
MFV 87	fishery protection	1944	50	–	6.3.57	–	–
Resold for commercial service, operating as *Grey Kelpir*, 1968.							
MOB 13	tanker	1946	136	–	15.4.57	–	–
Bt from RASC, then resold 15.4.57 Everard as *Totality*. Bu 1970.							
MMS 1061	motor minesweeper	1945	–	360	30.7.57	–	–
Resold 7.57							
Crouch	RASC fast launch	1945	–	8	31.7.57	–	–
Resold via Hilsea depot.							
Dee	RASC fast launch	1945	–	8	31.7.57	–	–
Resold via Hilsea depot.							
Nettle	torpedo recovery	1933	–	222	14.8.57	–	91, 92
Still afloat as *Elfin*. For full story, see text.							
NA 13	armament lighter		–	–	27.11.57	1,275	–
Bisham	inshore minesweeper	1954	–	129	1957	–	49, 57
Full story for *Bisham* and next two minesweepers in text.							

Name	Type	Built	GRT	Displnt	Bought	Cost (£)	Text ref
Broadley	inshore minesweeper	1953	–	123	1957	–	49, 57, 115, 116
Edlingham	inshore minesweeper	1955	–	129	1957	–	49, 57
Reigate	gate vessel	1918	–	300	c. 1958	–	–
Falconet	boom defence vessel	1939	–	605	1958	–	–
Martinet	boom defence vessel	1939	–	605	1958	–	–
Planet	boom defence vessel	1939	–	695	1958	–	–
Signet	boom defence vessel	1939	–	605	1958	–	–
Emulous	tug	1942	129	–	25.3.58	–	–
Resold for commercial use in Canada 1961 as *Irving Oak*. Scuttled 1991.							
TID 61	tug	1945	54	–	9.4.58	–	–
Resold for commercial use in Canada 1961.							
Baritone	boom defence vessel	1945	–	730	14.5.58	–	–
Barbrook	boom defence vessel	1938	–	750	14.5.58	–	–
Barberry	boom defence vessel	1943	–	750	14.5.58	–	–
Bownet	boom defence vessel	1939	–	605	14.5.58	–	–
Rodwell	trial/cable lighter	–	–	–	10.6.58	1,775	–
Former *X216*, Bu by Pounds.							
Proud Knight	MTB	1945	–	44	18.6.58	–	–
Resold probably by 8.58.							
Proud Lancer	MTB	1946	–	44	18.6.58	–	29
Resold.							
Proud Highlander	MTB	1945	–	44	18.6.58	–	29
Resold.							
Barilla	boom defence vessel	1943	–	750	23.7.58	–	–
Egerton	tug	1943	203	–	29.7.58	–	–
Former *Empire Darby*. Resold as *Irving Beech*, 1961, Canada. Wrecked 12.67.							
Alligator	naval tug	1941	630	–	1.8.58	–	–
Ex-*Charon*. Resold for commercial service as *Irving Birch*.							
RN Air 1F	aircraft lighter	–	–	350	31.8.58	4,175	–
Former *LCT 1012*.							
Assiduous	naval tug	1943	597	–	10.9.58	–	–
Resold as *Irving Tamarack*, 1961, Canada.							
Sir Walter Campbell	RASC coaster	1928	434	–	27.10.58	–	–
Wave Conqueror	oiler	1953	8,187	–	12.58	–	–
Resold for oil storage, Le Havre then Bu La Spezia, 4.60.							
TID 46	tug	1943	54	–	9.1.59	–	–
Wave King	oiler	1944	8,159	–	3.6.59	–	–
Resold BISCO for £65,000 then Bu T.W. Ward, Barrow, arriving 16.4.60.							
Useful	tug	1935	58	–	10.11.59	650	–
Industrious	paddle tug	1902	403	–	25.11.59	–	–
Towed to IJmuiden, Netherlands, 5.12.59 for Bu.							
Wave Monarch	tanker	1944	8,181	–	3.1.60	–	–
Sold for oil storage at Le Havre as *Noema*, replacing *Wave Conqueror*, then Bu Spain 1964.							
Sprite	naval tug	1915	412	–	14.3.60	–	–
Resold for Bu Rotterdam, arrived there 27.3.60.							
Pilot	tug	1909	403	–	17.3.60	–	–
Resold with *Sprite* for Bu Rotterdam.							
TID 50	tug	1943	54	–	25.3.60	–	70
Survived at Pounds until at least 1983, but Bu by 1990.							
Maryston	cargo	1920	435	–	4.1.60	–	–
Resold 8.1960 for Bu by Dutch interests.							
YC 76	mooring lighter	1960	–	–	29.6.60	2,389	–
Resold Netherlands for Bu 1962.							
Aid	dockyard tug	1945	274	–	26.7.60	–	–
Former *Empire Jenny*, resold for commercial use in Canada as *Irving Teak*.							
Empire Imp	tug	1942	129	–	1.8.60	–	–
Resold 1962 as *Irving Walnut* to Canada, scuttled 1969.							
C621	stores lighter	1944	192	–	9.8.60	7,347	–
Resold to Dutch breakers, but then further service as *Maureen Brush*.							
Britannic	tug/cable barge	1941	346	–	9.8.60	2,347	–
Probably ex-*Miner V*. Resold to Dutch breakers who resold to Bush for £1,000 4.62.							

Name	Type	Built	GRT	Displnt	Bought	Cost (£)	Text ref
Minion	tug	1940	56	–	19.8.60	–	–
Ex-Priddy's Hard.							
X 140	cable lighter	1915	130	–	23.8.60	844	–
Ex-landing barge X-lighter.							
TRC 17	torpedo recovery	1942	–	–	23.8.60	587	–
Ex-German *Jaeger* class, prize in 1945 at end of war.							
TID 75	tug	1944	54	–	10.10.60	–	–
Resold for commercial use and sank in Bay of Biscay, 1996.							
TID 76	tug	1944	54	–	18.10.60	–	–
Bu at Pounds.							
LCM (7) 7146	landing craft	1945	28	–	19.12.60	–	–
Statesman	submarine	1943	–	715	3.1.61	–	36, 83 111, 116
Bu mid-1970s.							
YC 97	mooring lighter	1911	–	–	21.2.61	–	–
VIC 79	stores carrier	1945	124	–	20.4.61	2,281	–
Sold to Taylor Chatham for further service.							
VIC 54	stores carrier	1946	124	–	20.4.61	2,079	–
TID 71	tug	1944	54	–	28.6.61	220	–
Resold Husbands Shipyard for further commercial use.							
VIC 59	stores carrier	–	–	–	1961	–	–
Resold 7.5.62 to Turner and Hickman for £2,850.							
Mersey no. 44	light vessel	1880	184	–	9.12.61	–	–
Former *Planet* of Mersey Docks & Harbour Board, resold for Bu at VHF Belgium for £11,000, 3.64.							
Harle	trawler	1947	506	–	1961	–	–
Resold VHF Belgium presumed for Bu.							
Weather Observer	weather ship	1940	–	950	1961	–	72
Resold VHF for Bu 9.61 for £14,000. Ex-Flower corvette HMS *Marguerite*, converted to weather ship at Sheerness, 1947.							
Myles Kennedy	bucket dredger	1921	413	–	22.2.62	6,250	27
Resold to Metrec interests 5.68, quite possibly for use as a crane barge in HMS *Drake* salvage project off Rathlin Island, Northern Ireland.							
Hilsea	ferry	1930	149	–	26.2.62	1,750	–
Resold for commercial service to Doeksen Salvage Co, Den Helder, Netherlands, and used on ferry service to Terschelling, then Bu 1967 at Den Helder.							
Wootton	ferry	1928	150	–	26.2.62	1,750	–
Worked on Portsmouth–Fishbourne route, 1928–61, except for period as minesweeper during the Second World War. Present at Dunkirk, 1940. Resold to Flandria, Netherlands, in 1964, used as fireboat then ferry again. Bu 2015.							
Exhorter	tug	1942	539	–	10.5.62	5,790	–
Resold for £12,705 for further service in Malta as *Bezzina Malta*. Towed from Portsmouth 21.12.63.							
Barcroft	boom defence	1939	–	730	30.5.62	5,579	–
Resold 1964 to Metrec interests. Bu Scrappingco, 1965.							
Barcock	boom defence	1941	–	730	30.5.62	7,277	–
Used to dismantle Southsea submarine defences.							
Moorfield	mooring vessel	1941	650	–	30.5.62	6,609	–
Bu at Pounds.							
YC 112	mooring lighter	1944	–	–	12.6.62	3,588	–
Alarm	light vessel	1913	247	–	7.62	–	–
Ex-Mersey Docks and Harbour Board.							
Barcastle	boom defence	1938	–	730	24.10.62	5,319	–
Barbette	boom defence	1943	–	730	24.10.62	6,285	–
Resold as *Fair Barbette*, 1964. Bu Belgium, 1965.							
Hercules	floating crane	1901	652	–	1962	–	–
Towed from Liverpool, July 1962. Resold Zeebrugge, 1963 for £9,000.							
YC 76	yard craft	–	–	–	1962	–	–
Resold Netherlands.							
No 43	light vessel	–	–	–	1962	6,480	–
Bt from Kellocks, possibly resold to Stephenson £5,900.							
Bold Pathfinder	MGB	1951	–	150	1962	–	36, 40
Had revolutionary gas turbine propulsion. Resold Naples interests and then Bt back without engines.							
Skua	aircraft transport	1945	–	990	21.5.62	–	–
Ex-*Walrus*. Resold as *Astragate*. Bu Sittingbourne, 1984.							

Name	Type	Built	GRT	Displnt	Bought	Cost (£)	Text ref
Leadsman	coastal tanker	1944	402	–	1962	4,500	–
Ex-*Chant II*, Resold for commercial use in Malta to S. Bezzina. Bu Spain 1974.							
Eddybay	oiler	1952	2,156	–	2.7.63	26,670	29
Bu Antwerp from 29.8.64. Presumed Pounds sold her to Antwerp breakers.							
C1	Admiralty coal hulk	1904	7,000	–	2.9.63	19,100	59, 60
Resold Hendrik-Ido-Ambacht, Netherlands, for Bu. Left Portsmouth 15.1.64.							
Destiny	tug	1937	91	–	25.9.63	4,080	–
Built as *Oner II* in 1937, Bt by Admiralty in 1938 and renamed *C10* and then *Destiny* (1958). Distinguished war service including involvement in D-Day, laying Pluto pipeline, and moving Mulberry Harbour units. Pounds resold as *Affluence* to Husbands. Then had several owners and, was last reported to being restored at Sharpness.							
C654	lub oil lighter	–	–	–	1.11.63	280	–
No 25	concrete barge	–	–	–	1.11.63	110	–
Lurcher	coaster	–	859	–	5.11.63	–	–
Ex-*Yewmount*. Resold T.W. Ward, Preston, for £3,375 and arrived there for Bu 31.3.64.							
No 26	concrete barge				15.11.63	110	–
Possibly this concrete barge and those below were acquired to assist with land reclamation at Pounds' Tipner site, although one was resold for £1,100 in 1.1964							
No 28	concrete barge	–	–	–	15.11.63	110	–
No 32	concrete barge	–	–	–	15.11.63	110	–
No 33	concrete barge	–	–	–	15.11.63	110	–
No 34	concrete barge	–	–	–	15.11.63	110	–
No 47	concrete barge	–	–	–	15.11.63	110	–
No 50	concrete barge	–	–	–	15.11.63	110	–
C655	stores lighter	–	–	–	15.11.63	1,638	–
Resold Belgium/Netherlands for Bu.							
Fylde	bucket dredger	1938	465	–	27.11.63	–	–
Bt from T.W. Ward, shipbreakers with *Rossall* (see next entry) for £10,500, 29.11.63. Resold John Brown, 20.3.64 for £9,850.							
Rossall	grab dredger	1921	239	–	29.11.63	–	23
Bt from T.W. Ward with *Fylde* for £10,500 29.11.63. Bu post-1969?							
Trunnion	tug	1938	178	–	30.12.63	1,638	–
Formerly based at Plymouth. Resold for Bu in Belgium or Netherlands.							
Peter Joliffe	tug	1940	80	–	12.12.63	–	–
Resold Tees 3.64 for £1,500, after being used by Pounds as a tug.							
C666	stores lighter	–	–	–	27.1.64	410	–
Kathleen and May	schooner	1900	136	–	30.1.64	1,500	76
Bt from Boughton, resold quickly for £1,750. Famous schooner, now preserved at Gloucester.							
YC 389	mooring lighter	1946	–	–	31.7.64	–	–
RN Air 2F	aircraft lighter	1944	–	–	14.8.64	9,000	–
Former *LCT 1138*. £9,000 cost includes *C21* and *YC 389*.							
C21	sullage lighter	1872	140	–	14.8.64	–	44, 49 50, 51
Used as a crane barge around Tipner until at least late 1970s. Then Bu 1985. Built as HMS *Fidget* 1872, a flat iron gunboat.							
Unknown	re dock'	–	–	–	21.8.64	22,500	–
Unclear what this relates to, possibly 'Mulberry Harbour' section used for land reclamation in East Yard.							
C645	stores lighter	1940	–	–	8.64	468	–
Min alternative name.							
Interknit	dumb tank cleaning vessel		–	–	1.10.64	2,000	–
Ex-*LCS (R)*. Bt from R. & H. Green and Silley Weir Ltd.							
Tolverne	grab hopper dredger	1929	164	–	19.11.64	2,000	–
Bt from Metrec interests.							
Foulney	grab hopper dredger	1938	633	–	1964	–	–
Resold Scrappingco, Antwerp, 1964, for Bu.							
C11	coal hulk	1932	–	–	1964	–	–
Bt back from British Rail to whom Pounds had sold her in 1954. Ultimate fate unknown.							
YC 3034	cooking lighter	–	–	–	1964	160	–
C619	stores lighter	1943	181	–	24.5.65	1	–
Resold Oyster Bay shipyard Weymouth, 7.66.							
Tongham	cable lighter	1938	70	–	25.5.65	338	68
Resold for commercial use.							
Ben Olliver	converted tanker	–	–	–	4.8.65	4,219	–
Resold 12.1965 as suction dredger. Sank 1969 off Langstone Bar.							

Name	Type	Built	GRT	Displnt	Bought	Cost (£)	Text ref
C620	stores lighter	1944	192	–	2.9.65	–	–
Resold for commercial use.							
Drakedene	motor ship	1946	419	–	10.9.65	5,000	–
Resold 1966 to K. Perrakis Piraeus as *Vivian G* for £7,000.							
Sea Devil	submarine	1945	–	715	18.10.65	–	–
Resold to Metrec interests at Newhaven for Bu, left 15.12.65.							
MRC 1015	Maintenance and Repair craft	1944	–	500	1965	–	55
Ex-LCT Mark 3. LCT *7065*. Seen at Pounds 9.65.							
MRC 1098	Maintenance and Repair craft	1942	–	500	1965	–	–.
Ex-LCT Mark 4. LCT *382*. Seen at Pounds 9.65.							
F.W.31	dumb barge	1948	126	–	1965	50	–.
C674	harbour launch	1944	26	–	21.1.66	–	–
Former *HL(S)306*. Resold became *Gugh* of Isles of Scilly, seen at Hull Marina, 2011.							
F.W.32	dumb barge	1948	126	–	23.6.66	50	–
Bt from Corralls.							
F.W.37	dumb barge	1948	126	–	23.6.66	50	–
Chattenden	armament carrier	1944	322	–	23.6.66	–	–
Resold 1968 as dredger *Mark Bowen*, then Bu Northam from 1979.							
Rampisham	inshore minesweeper	1957	–	120	16.8.66	–	–
Resold Italian interests for £2,000.							
Zealous	motor vessel	1948	19		18.8.66	450	–
Pulham	inshore minesweeper	1956	–	120	19.8.66	–	–
Reedham	inshore minesweeper	1958	–	120	29.9.66	–	–
Resold for commercial use in Mediterranean as MY *Marisa*.							
Woldingham	inshore minesweeper	1957	–	120	29.9.66	–	–
Resold for use in Mediterranean.							
Bold Pathfinder	fast patrol boat	1951	–	150	29.9.66	2,000	–
Bt back from Naples interests to whom she was sold in 1962 and who had extracted engine. Finally Bu 1985.							
Sir Montagu	tug	1936	61	–	13.10.66	–	–
Resold for further service in Greece.							
Pompey Light	collier	1949	1,428	–	14.10.66	16,000	–
Resold Jos de Smedt, Antwerp, for Bu, which began 10.68.							
Cranham	inshore minesweeper	1954	–	120	28.10.66	–	–
Resold W.T. Hunt, then commercial use in Adriatic as *Fulgidas*.							
Bassingham	inshore minesweeper	1953	–	120	1966	4,888	37
Bu 29.8.80 to 10.10.80.							
TID 32	tug	1943	54	–	27.1.67	388	–
Former *C.702*. Bu from 1967 but remains still visible 1988.							
Effra	collier	1946	2,701	–	27.1.67	22,000	–
Resold to Greek buyers for £25,000 4.67 as *Yannakis Fanis*. Bu 1974.							
Vacesay	MS trawler	1945	443	–	21.3.67	5,388	–
Towed 7.67 from Rosyth by tug *Tradesman*. Resold Bakkers, Bruges, for Bu, left 9.5.68.							
VWL 10	water lighter	1945	143	–	29.3.67	920	–
Ex-*MOB 3*.							
N.S.C.(L) 104	generator lighter	1943	–	350	5.4.67	6,888	–
Former *LCT 472*.							
Abbotsham	inshore minesweeper	1957	–	120	16.5.67	–	–
Resold.							
Rackham	inshore minesweeper	1956	–	120	17.8.67	7,537	43, 67
Reported to have left Pounds in 1979 for Bu elsewhere.							
Sidlesham	inshore minesweeper	1955	–	120	17.8.67	–	–
Resold for commercial use, first as police training ship *Gerald Daniel* at Chichester. From 1985 used as Christian centre, then from 2010 to date moored on Thames. Sank 2025.							
Dingley	inshore minesweeper	1953	–	123	17.8.67	–	–
Bu Pounds, 1977.							
Shell-Mex 3	tanker	1921	128	–	1.9.67	1,500	–
Resold 1970.							
Airmoor 11	RAF Moorings Vessel	1943	178	–	15.9.67	–	–
Former *MMS 256*. Resold for commercial use to Folkestone Salvage as *Kay Belle*.							
Marlingford	seaward defence boat	1956	–	120	19.10.67	1,200	–
Bt at Singapore and disposed of locally there.							
Scotscraig	Tay ferry	1951	463	–	12.1967	7,500	61, 63
Both *Scotscraig* and *Abercraig* made redundant by opening of Tay Road Bridge. Resold to Malta for commercial service.							

Name	Type	Built	GRT	Displnt	Bought	Cost (£)	Text ref
Abercraig	Tay ferry	1939	445	–	12.1967	7,500	–
Tilford	seaward defence boat	1958	–	120	1967	–	–
Resold at Singapore.							
Premier	tug	1900	52	–	1968	–	–
Resold to Bowen and Caines, then bought back.							
TID 68	tug	1944	54	–	1968	–	–
Reported Bu at Pounds.							
Floriston	coastal minesweeper	1955	–	360	7.6.68	–	–
Was to be converted to floating crane, seen at Pounds 1975, ultimate fate unclear.							
Blackburn	RNR accommodation ship, formerly aircraft transport	1946	705	–	24.7.68		
Resold 1972 as *Harpounds* for £10,834 for commercial use. *Gardline Locater* from 1975, Bu 1997.							
M.S.C. Mallard	tug	1940	131	–	27.9.68	1,000	–
Resold 1970 to Metrec interests. Various owners then Bu Millom, 1985.							
M.S.C. Merlin	tug	1940	131	–	27.9.68	1,000	–
Resold for commercial service. Reported Bu Aliaga, Turkey, 2015.							
NA 151	armament carrier	1941	100	–	28.10.68	–	–
Brigham	inshore minesweeper	1953	–	120	20.12.68	–	–
Resold 12.69 to Australian Marine Ind Pty.							
W33	hopper barge	–	444	–	3.2.69	1,500	50
Pick-me-up	dredger	1902	170	–	12.3.69	415	–
Ex-British Railways Board.							
YC 465	lighter	–	–	–	2.5.69	–	–
August Bebel	East German trawler	1950	261	–	12.6.69	3,147	72
Sold for £8,500 to Mellenger of Canada 28.10.69. Various other owners, last reported as detained in South Africa.							
Anton Saefkow	East German trawler	1950	257	–	12.6.69	3,147	72
Reported 1972 as *Misty Fox* (?). Deleted Lloyds Register, 1997.							
Rostock	East German trawler	1951	257	–	12.6.69	3,147	72
Sold for £4,000 to Bull of Newhaven, 8.8.69. Various future owners and reported Bu Gillingham, 1979.							
Max Reimann	East German trawler	1950	257	–	12.6.69	3,147	72
Resold for future service and reported Bu UK, 1979.							
Wolgograd	East German trawler	1950	256	–	12.6.69	3,147	72
Former *Stalingrad*. Resold for future service and sank, 1979.							
Klara Zetkin	East German trawler	1950	257	–	12.6.69	3,147	72
Resold for future service and deleted Lloyds Register, 1999.							
Heinrich Mann	East German trawler	1949	255	–	12.6.69	3,147	72
Resold to Greek owners and sank, 1974.							
Erich Honecker	East German trawler	1951	257	–	12.6.69	3,147	72
Sold for £7,500 to Melleneger of Canada 23.12.69. Last reported in existence 2002.							
Karl Liebknecht	East German trawler	–	–	–	17.7.69	3,467	72
Sold to Hamburg owners and deleted from Lloyds Register 1974.							
YC 3030	cooking lighter	–	–	–	23.8.69	238	–
Gatling	armament carrier	1945	–	391	10.10.69	3,688	–
Bu Passage West, Ireland, 1970.							
C611	separator lighter	1942	100	–	17.10.69	–	–
Tsefat	merchant	1959	1,346	–	18.11.69	35,200	–
The ship had been badly damaged by fire and explosion at Rotterdam 15.4.69 before Pounds purchase. Resold for £60,000 14.12.69 to Passer.							
Dogfish	LCT (3)	–	–	500	5.12.69	18,506	–
Vosper VT1	hovercraft	–	–	–	5.12.69	–	–
Vosper VT1M	hovercraft	–	–	–	5.12.69	–	–
Plaboy	tug	1957	36	–	1970	–	–
Resold for £11,850 to Commercial Bank of Near East, Greece, 11.71.							
Plastron	tug	1953	80	–	1970	–	–
Ex-P.L.A. Resold 12.71 South Ocean Services for £1,000. Wrecked Cornwall, 1973.							
Crane Lighter No.1	floating crane	–	–	–	1970	–	–
Tyr	Danish landing craft	1963	315	–	1970	–	48
Refurbished, then sold 1975 Plessey as *Sono* for £20,000 then to Turner, Guernsey.							
Uller	Danish landing craft	–	–	–	1970	–	–
Brage	Danish landing craft	–	–	–	1970	–	–
Token	submarine	1943	–	1,090	1970	–	–
Resold Shipbreaking (Queenborough) Ltd for Bu Cairnryan 2.70.							

Name	Type	Built	GRT	Displnt	Bought	Cost (£)	Text ref
YC 3029	cooking lighter	–	–	–	3.4.70	268	43
Fitted with a crane and used in demolition of frigate *Volage*.							
TID 73	tug	–	–	–	3.4.70	–	–
Named *Dashound* for a while. Presumed Bu by Pounds.							
Portcullis	LCT (8)	1946	–	657	15.5.70	–	–
Former *LCT 4044*. Resold for commercial service as *Island Spruce* 1973. Wrecked 1974.							
Citadel	LCT (8)	1945	–	657	15.6.70	–	46
Former *LCT 4038*. Resold 3.11.71 for commercial use in Italy to Paul Murri for £18,026 (US$45,000).							
NA 149	armament lighter	1940	100	–	15.6.70	–	–
NA 46	armament lighter	–	–	–	26.6.70	–	49
Removed to Tipner 19.8.70.							
NA 165	armament carrier	1941	100	–	26.6.70	–	–
Resold for commercial use.							
Lanyard	armament carrier	1938	221	–	26.6.70	–	–
Spa	water tank vessel	1942	719	–	26.6.70	–	–
Resold Haulbowline Industries for Bu 1970.							
Salisbury	US special survey ship	1944	6,108	–	22.9.70	50,550	72
Ex-*Defiance*, ex-*Helen Lykes*. US ship type C2-5-B1. Bt as lying in Seychelles for US$120,880 via Crown Agents. Reported as resold for demolition in Singapore, 1971.							
TRC 15	torpedo recovery	–	–	–	29.10.70	–	–
Both this and TRC 14 below were prizes taken at end of war. Ex-German *Jaeger* class.							
TRC 14	torpedo recovery	–	–	–	31.12.70	–	–
Tulagi	tug	1954	54	–	31.12.70	–	–
Resold for £3,000 to Port Talbot and Marine. Reported then abandoned on River Bandon, County Cork, Ireland, from 2006.							
VIC 77	stores lighter	1945	147	–	1971	–	–
Resold for commercial use. Resold as *Victual*.							
NSC(L)108	naval servicing craft	–	–	–	26.2.71	–	–
Former *LCT (4) 1306*, resold to Djibouti for £25,000.							
TCC Hopper No 3	hopper	1956	658	–	26.2.71	15,000	65
Resold J.J. Beddows, 1974.							
TCC Hopper No 5	hopper	1950	751	–	18.5.71	15,000	–
Resold Haulbowline, 1974, then Spain.							
TCC Hopper No 6	hopper	1950	751	–	18.5.71	15,000	–
Resold J.J. Beddows, 1974.							
Leverton	coastal minesweeper	1955	–	360	14.5.71	–	64, 65, 116
Resold for Bu Willments, Southampton, 1977.							
Boston Valetta	trawler	1956	239	–	18.5.71	6,500	–
From Boston Deep Sea Fishing. Resold as *Lady Cora*.							
Tiptoe	submarine	1944	–	1310	8.6.71	–	43, 48, 84, 85, 86
Bu East Yard by 1992, after long lay on Pounds' moorings.							
Kemerton	coastal minesweeper	1953	–	360	13.8.71	15,500	–
Bt from Metrec interests, towed Poole for Bu 1975							
Brearley	inshore minesweeper	1955	–	123	25.10.71	–	–
Resold for commercial use.							
August	unknown		–	–	2.11.71	–	–
Evdelos	coaster	1955	892	–	15.11.71	17,200	–
Ex-*Essex Coast*. Resold Pothitos, Malta, for further service 1972. Bu Greece, 1985.							
Chilcompton	coastal minesweeper	1954	–	360	23.11.71	–	–
Resold Metrec interests, Newhaven, for Bu.							
Towing Wizard	tug	1955	122	–	26.11.71	–	70
Ex-*Quaysider*. Sank 11.71, was refloated by Pounds. Then used as a tug before being resold for further service in Greece, 1978. Wrecked 2002.							
Fiskerton	coastal minesweeper	1958	–	360	1971	10,432	65, 115
Resold for Bu Dartford 1977 by Henderson Morez.							
Hercules	floating crane	–	–	–	1971	6,450	–
Bt from Vamvoungkis, resold 12.5.71 for £9,950.							
Tigris	tug	–	–	–	1971	–	–
Resold 6.1971.							
Kendiken	tug	1954	200	–	1972	–	71
Swansea tug *Wallasey* renamed *Kendiken* 1972. Resold Willments. Bu 1993?							

Name	Type	Built	GRT	Displnt	Bought	Cost (£)	Text ref
Panagia	dredger	1954	2,588	–	*c.* 1972	–	–
Resold Somalia as *Agia Irene*, 12.73.							
Bastion	LCT (8)	1945	–	657	*c.* 1972	–	47
Ex-LCT *4040*. Left by 1976, presumed to be resold.							
Akyab	LCT (8)	1946	–	657	*c.* 1972	28,880	–
Ex-LCT *4037*. Resold for £52,762 (including spares and repairs) for commercial use in Madagascar.							
Salveda	salvage vessel	1943	–	1,250	2.1.72	–	–
Eventful wartime career. Towed HMS *Warspite* in Mediterranean after she was hit by glider bomb in 1943. Sold to G. Vamvoounakis Piraeus, 11.72.							
Demon	floating crane	1883	–	508	3.72	1,240	40, 41, 42, 114, 115
Ex-gunboat *Handy*. Eventful career and ultimately dismantled at Pounds. See text for full details.							
Artemis	submarine	1947	–	1,120	1972	23,844	43, 84, 85, 86, 115, 117
Lu for many years at Pounds' moorings, Bu early 1990s.							
Moorsman	mooring vessel	1945	–	1,000	6.6.72	13,232	–
Harrogate	cargo ship	1959	963	–	26.6.72	24,650	–
Resold 1972 for £24,100 for commercial use, renamed *Dimitris*, wrecked 1991.							
Seamoor	mooring vessel	1942	–	225	28.6.72	2,388	–
Former *MMS 86*, resold for commercial use as *Celtic Lord* and Bu Inverkeithing, 1982.							
YC 327	cooking lighter	1954	200	–	27.7.72	2,688	–
Resold 3.76 to Haulbowline Industries, Ireland.							
C99	lighter	–	–	–	27.7.72	1,188	–
Resold Willments for £2,000.							
VIC 33	stores carrier	1944	96	–	6.72	–	83
Called *Smeaton* for a while from 1951.							
Shell Welder	coastal tanker	1959	569	–	2.10.72	15,000	–
Resold 1972 Northwood (Fareham) Ltd for £20,000, converted to sand dredger and renamed *Steel Welder*. Bu 1991.							
Volage	frigate	1943	–	2,240	11.10.72	32,380	43, 44, 45, 49, 114, 116
Arrived 1973 at Pounds and gradually Bu. Remains of hull still visible off East Yard at low tide at time of going to press.							
Puncheston	coastal minesweeper	1957	–	360	28.10.72	–	65, 115
Resold Henderson Morez, Dartford, for Bu. Already a hulk when left Pounds, 4.77.							
Cannon	tug	1943	91	–	15.5.72	–	–
Selby	coaster	1959	962	–	9.10.72	31,000	–
Resold 29.3.73, as *Raven*.							
Dalswinton	coastal minesweeper	1954	–	360	11.11.72	12,288	–
Resold Willments, Southampton, for Bu, 1977.							
C112	lub oil lighter	1941	182	–	1.3.73	2,680	–
Portcullis	degaussing vessel	1946	–	657	30.4.73	–	–
Former LCT *4044*.							
TID 99	tug	1944	54	–	31.5.73	1,038	–
Bu or hulked Pounds *c.* 1979.							
Tanac 35	tug	1944	67	–	1.11.73	1,188	–
Sank, refloated, and sold 1977. Tanac tugs were built in Canada from 1944.							
SWBC 1	shallow water boom craft	1943	–	–	8.74	–	–
Former LCT *(3) 433*. Sold Captain Fusco, Sardinia, 6.75 for £37,000.							
Alcide	submarine	1945	–	1,120	1974	–	–
Resold Drapers Hull for Bu, arrived there 7.8.74.							
Belton	coastal minesweeper	1957	–	360	1974	–	–
Resold Spanish breakers at Gijon 1974.							
Shell Farmer	coastal tanker	1955	313	–	1974?	–	–
Resold Metrec interests for £21,000, 2.75. Renamed *Coast Farmer*.							
LCF 34	landing craft flak	1943	–	420	1975	–	46, 47, 114, 116
Ex-LCT *701*. Bu 1990. Bt from Vernons of Chichester.							
Zeebrugge	LST (3) 3532	1945	–	2,256	1975	–	–
Resold Spanish breakers at Gijon, direct from Devonport.							
RTTL	RAF target tower	–	–	–	by 1975	–	–
C 708	ex-VIC lighter	1944	147	–	by 1975	–	–
Former *VIC 54*, Bu at Pounds, 1975.							
Algol	Dutch pilot cutter	1950	432	–	2.75	–	–
Resold 16.9.76 to Druid Hurst Australia who resold for £20,000 to be *Lord Amory*, scout project ship, in West India Dock, London, where she remains.							

Name	Type	Built	GRT	Displnt	Bought	Cost (£)	Text ref
Aldebaran	Dutch pilot cutter	–	–	–	2.75	–	–
	Resold for £20,468 for commercial use to Puerto Rican interests.						
Sand Finch	suction dredger	1958	478	–	27.2.75	9,600	–
	Ex-*Ron Woolaway*. Resold 1.78 for US$39,982 to Frangoulis as *Lacky* and then *Triena*.						
BP Haulier	tanker	1955	315	–	28.2.75	15,000	–
	Resold for US$44,000 to Hadjifotis for commercial use in Greece as *Chrissanthy X*, 1977.						
GE2	floating grain elevator	1954	403	–	9.5.75	23,220	–
	Former *MOT Elevator No 4* at Bristol. Pontoon survived at Tipner until 1980s at least.						
Texas	LCT	Unknown	–	–	7.75	49,089	46
Lune Venture	trawler	1945	120	–	c. 1975	–	–
	Former MFV *1562*, then *Pakefield*. Resold by Pounds for commercial use.						
Coast Farmer	tanker	1955	313	–	c. 1975	–	114
	Resold, converted into sand dredger and Bu 1987.						
LC 17	lifting craft	1942	552	–	21.11.75	13,380	–
	From MOD. Sold Metrec interests 3.76 for £17,000. Then Cromarty Firth Eng, then to Nontox as *Chain Surveyor*.						
No 13	floating crane	–	–	–	9.12.75	27,280	–
Isle of Ely	freighter (BR)	1958	1,451	–	11.3.76	–	–
	Resold for commercial service 2.80 to Desio Shipping as *Spice Island*. Bu Bakkers, 1984.						
Saxon 11	tug?	–	–	–	5.3.76	7,094	–
	Bt from Kellock, resold for £10,000, 8.78.						
LC 19	lifting craft	1942	522	–	15.6.76	13,640	–
LC 16	lifting craft	1942	464	–	15.6.76	9,400	–
	Two of LC 16 and, LC 19 and LC 17 above, ex-MOD lifting craft were sold to Bakkers of Bruges for £35,184, presumably for Bu. The third was sold to Howard Doris for £22,000, 9.76.						
ASP 11	ASP	–	–	–	10.8.76	–	–
ASP 12	ASP	–	–	–	10.8.76	–	–
ASP 15	ASP	–	–	–	10.8.76		53
Arsella	Italian minesweeper	1955	–	119	5.4.76	16,388	64, 93, 94, 95
	Together with *Conchiglia* below were returned to US Navy who sold to Pounds. See p. 93 for their use in the film *The Greek Tycoon*.						
Conchiglia	Italian minesweeper	1955	–	119	5.4.76	16,388	64, 93, 94, 95
Acacia	Italian minesweeper	1953	–	378	7.4.1976	19,000	–
	Returned to US Navy who then sold to Pounds.						
Ciliego	Italian Minesweeper	1953	–	378	7.4.1976	19,000	–
	Returned to US Navy who then sold to Pounds.						
Beemster	coastal minesweeper	1953	–	360	8.4.76	14,669	–
	Together with the three minesweepers below, transferred from the US Navy to the Royal Netherlands Navy in 1953/4. Seen at Southampton in 1976 so likely to have been Bu at Willments or sold for further service.						
Borculo	coastal minesweeper	1953	–	360	8.4.76	14,669	–
Borne	coastal minesweeper	1953	–	360	8.4.76	14,669	–
Brielle	coastal minesweeper	1953	–	360	8.4.76	14,669	–
Montezuma III	US tug	1941	237	–	6.75	61,500	–
	Sold 6.76 to Greek interests. Bu 1998.						
Paul Holme	dredger	1961	900	–	30.7.76	55,000	–
	Resold Northwood Fareham for £73,000.						
Pero Escobar	Portuguese frigate	1957	–	1,279	14.9.76	8,022	–
	Presumed to have been Bu in Portugal.						
Dufton	coastal minesweeper	1955	–	360	7.10.76	18,888	–
	Resold Liguria Maritime, Sittingbourne, 1976, for Bu.						
Lord Ritchie	tug	1959	109	–	12.76	55,000	70, 71, 94
	Resold for commercial use1985, having been used by Pounds as a tug and for films.						
Topmast 18	salvage vessel	1943	424	–	24.12.76	19,500	46, 48, 114
	Former *LCT (3)*. Reacquired following 1965 sale to Risdon Beazley. Fire in 1978 led to further conversion work being halted. Bu Bakkers Bruges.						
Eidechse	landing craft	1945	–	743	1976	–	46
	Former German Navy and ex-USS *LSM 491* resold by Pounds as *Hodeidah* then *Ocean Bay* for further commercial services with Ocean Offshore Services, Guernsey.						
Krokodil	landing craft	1945	–	743	1976	–	46, 47
	Ex-German Navy and USS *LSM 537D*. Resold by Pounds for £70,000 as *Ocean Beach* in 1977 with Ocean Offshore Services, Guernsey. Bu 2005.						
Attinia	inshore minesweeper	1955	–	119	1976	–	–
	Ex-Italian Navy, resold.						

Name	Type	Built	GRT	Displnt	Bought	Cost (£)	Text ref
Calamaro	inshore minesweeper	1955	–	119	1976	–	–
Ex-Italian Navy, resold.							
Thakeham	inshore minesweeper	1957	–	120	1977	–	67
Resold for £15,600 in 2.80 as Greek ferry *Petrakis* at Corfu.							
Miner II	diving tender	1943	–	346	18.2.77	–	–
Resold Liguria Maritime Sittingbourne for Bu 9.1977.							
Miner III	diving tender	1940	–	346	3.3.77	3,840	–
Bt from MOD at Portland, possibly sold 1977 to Liguria Maritime for Bu.							
Manifour	hopper barge	1968	594	–	25.3.77	9,250	–
Bt from/through Padstow Boating. Sold for £22,000, 1977.							
2	amphibious LARCs	–	–	–	13.5.77	21,336	–
Hjaelperen	Danish depot ship	1945	–	743	1977	–	46, 48
Former US LSM-500, transferred to Royal Danish Navy. Resold by Pounds, 1982 for Bu, Southampton.							
Weather Surveyor	weather ship	1943	–	1,402	7.7.77	25,380	72
Former HMS *Rushen Castle*. Left 11.5.82 for Rijsdijk, Hendrik-Ido-Ambacht for Bu.							
Weather Reporter	weather ship	1944	–	1,358	1977	–	–
Former HMS *Oakham Castle*. Resold Tees Marine for Bu Middlesbrough, arrived there 21.11.77.							
Hoveringham	dredger	1956	120	–	1977	12,000	–
Bt from Liverpool, sold to Bowen and Cains for £28,000, 6.77.							
Samson	tug	1954	850	–	29.4.77	28,380	–
Resold for commercial use, left 24.12.1977 as *Cosmo* then Bu Italy, 1981.							
Mount Everest	trawler	1955	303	–	6.77	15,000	73
Bu 7.81 maybe not at Pounds.							
Joe Croan	trawler	1956	273	–	6.77	15,000	73
Resold for £14,000 to Bakkers Bruges for Bu, left 8.83.							
Lune Venture	trawler	1945	110	–	12.8.77	7,388	67
Repurchased and Bu at Pounds ultimately.							
LC 8	lifting craft	1940	938	–	20.11.77	20,328	–
Sold 6.78 for £20,000 to Belcon Shipping and Trading.							
LC 9	lifting craft	1940	938	–	25.11.77	20,000	–
Resold early 1980.							
LC 10	lifting craft	1940	918	–	c. 1977	–	–
Resold early 1980. Reported to be a pontoon jetty at Immingham, 2003.							
PTF 10	patrol craft	–	–	–	19.12.77	–	–
Former ex-USN Nasty class, resold 1980 for Bu.							
Blackburn Rovers	trawler	1962	439	–	12.6.78	12,000	–
Resold for £20,500 for commercial use in Mediterranean as *Giant Fish*.							
Spurs	trawler	1962	439	–	12.6.78	12,000	–
Resold for commercial use 1978 £20,500. Bu 1991 Bloors Wharf Medway.							
BJ Islander	safety standby	1952	341	–	19.9.77	22,000	–
Former US Bluebird minesweeper. Bu 6.1978.							
VA Islander	safety standby	1954	333	–	19.9.77	22,000	–
Former US Bluebird minesweeper converted and resold as luxury yacht *Alysse Maru*. Still in service.							
Abbeville	LCT (8)	1946	–	657	15.9.78	44,183	35
Ex-*LCT 4041*. Resold for commercial service as *Dolphin Carrier* then *Flying Comet*.							
Audemer	LCT (8)	1945	–	657	15.9.78	44,183	35, 46, 48
Ex-*LCT 4061*. Resold for commercial service as *Makola* and scuttled off Cameroon, 1985.							
Agheila	LCT (8)	1946	–	657	–	–	–
Ex-*LCT 4002*. Resold for commercial service as *Kwanda*.							
Al Khubar 3	Tug	1976	125	–	1978	–	–
Salvaged in Persian Gulf, arrived Camber 2.78, resold for commercial use.							
Unknown	floating crane	–	–	–	13.11.78	16,000	–
Flying Wizard	tug	1960	116	–	27.12.78	9,342	–
São Jorge	coastal minesweeper	1955	720		2.1979		64, 65
Former Portuguese minesweeper. Bt from Veitch, A.F. Ross and Sons, Girvan, who had laid her up at Cairnryan. Bu by 10.79.							
Hercules	tug	Unknown	–	–	1979	–	–
Resold 1979.							
Volesus	salvage vessel	Unknown	–	–	c. 1979	–	–
Ex-*Boston Fury*. Resold to H.K. Vickers.							
C617	lighter	1943	192	–	7.79	–	–
Resold for commercial use with Northwood (Fareham) Ltd.							

Name	Type	Built	GRT	Displnt	Bought	Cost (£)	Text ref
Grinder	dockyard tug	1958	472	–	6.12.79	21,882	–
Resold Spanish breakers Santander for £28,000, left 3.3.80.							
Griper	dockyard tug	1958	472	–	6.12.79	21,882	–
Resold Spanish breakers Santander for £28,000, left 26.2.80.							
Crave Bihen	trawler	–	–	–	4.1979	–	–
Stripped, beached Horsea for Bu by 1987.							
Kingfisher	houseboat ex-LCI (S)	1944	63	–	24.2.79	–	116
Lu many years in East Yard, hulked and reduced to aft half 6.90.							
Unknown	Tanac tug	–	–	–	15.8.79	3,182	–
DCI Perelle	sand dredger	1944	306	–	14.11.79	3,000	114
Former *LCT (3) Normandie*. Resold for Bu and had left by 31.8.84.							
Roger Grenville	catamaran	–	–	–	9.2.80	–	–
Used in *Mary Rose* expedition, had sunk twice in Camber. Unclear ultimate fate.							
Unknown	US patrol boat	–	–	–	15.2.80	24,978	–
Tongham	RNXS tender	1957		129	8.3.80	19,185	68
Resold to Pitchford 7.80 for £28,000. Became houseboat at Mistley 1996–2017. Now at Gillingham.							
LC 9	lifting craft	1940	938	–	14.3.80	16,000	–
Bought back from Teesside breakers.							
Steady	trials vessel	1944	–	346	21.3.80	5,388	–
Former *Miner VII*. Resold 1981 as Greek diving tender *Poseidon*.							
Bowstring	armament carrier	1938	220	–	26.3.80	1,868	50
Resold for Bu at an unknown location.							
Puttenham	RNXS tender	1958	–	120	20.5.80	19,185	–
Resold to Crete as ferry *Eletfheria*. Bu 2006.							
AFD 21	floating dock	1943	–	–	11.80	34,488	114, 115
Bt 11.80 but only left Rosyth for Pounds 26.8.81. Possibly resold Tanzania or Caymans, 1983.							
RG Masters VC	trials vessel	1954	–	170	17.11.80	7,188	67
Former *RAF 5002* and *Halsham*. Resold for further service in Greece as *Sotirakis*, 1981.							
Bucklesham	torpedo recovery	1954	–	120	1.12.80	–	–
Sold but quickly Bt back by Pounds (see later entry below).							
Cruiser	tug	1959	207	–	1980	15,000	–
Former *Clonmel*, resold Falmouth Towing as *St Gluvias*.							
Frome	hopper barge	1956	542	–	by 1981	–	–
Resold 1980 to Northwood (Fareham) Ltd.							
St Martin	MOD steam dredger	1951	390	–	5.3.81	–	–
Resold Bakkers, Bruges, for Bu, 1983.							
Bressuire	mooring hulk	1918	667	–	6.4.81	–	59
Bt from Sealink and resold Bakkers, Bruges, for Bu, 1981.							
Whimbrel	trials vessel	1944	481	–	29.5.81	13,364	–
Ex-LCT 7072. Resold Pierucci, 1982, but was to be repurchased in 1987.							
Repton	coastal minesweeper	1957	–	360	6.81	–	63, 116
Sold to Wake Metals 11.83 for £36,000, then Bu.							
Avon	MOD ramped powered lighter	1961	100	–	7.81	–	–
Resold as *Puffin Billy* 6.91 for further service in Persian Gulf.							
Bucklesham	inshore minesweeper	1954	–	120	1981	–	–
Resold 1989 as *Orca II*.							
Howitzer	armament carrier	1944	187	–	1981	–	114
Left 8.84 possibly for Bu Medway area.							
Barbara	tug	1963	91.5	–	16.7.82	–	–
Resold, became *Seamaid*. Sank on Thames, 2011.							
Isis	mine hunter	1955	–	123	10.8.82	5,336	114
Former *Cradley*, Bu by 1983.							
YC 477	cooking lighter	1958	133	–	9.82	–	52
Resold Hydro Seafood GSP Ltd Shetland for use on their fish farms.							
Gilmar	fishing vessel	1960	215	–	3.11.82	–	–
Resold for further fishing service to Harold Valman, Limehouse. Bu 1991.							
Kinellan	fishing vessel	1961	209	–	1982	–	–
Resold to Harold Valman for service at Milford Haven.							
Foylegarth	tug	1958	208	–	17.1.83	20,000	–
Resold Falmouth Towing, renamed *St Budoc* then *Foylegarth*, Bu New Holland 2010.							
Bonchurch	tug	1946	54	–	28.1.83	7,300	–
Former *TID 174*. Resold 1983 for £14,000 to Jersey interests for commercial use, last reported as houseboat on Mersey in 2018 and up for sale.							

Name	Type	Built	GRT	Displnt	Bought	Cost (£)	Text ref
Caldy	tank cleaning vessel	1943/	–	545	13.4.83	9,088	–
Resold Bakkers, Bruges, for Bu 5.83.							
Dee	seaward defence boat	1953	–	120	26.5.83	12,688	–
Former *Beckford*. Resold and given a three-mast schooner rig as bible ship *Beckford* (her original name). Bu Lowestoft 2017.							
Warmingham	inshore minesweeper	1956	–	120	1980	–	61
Resold as MV *Nautilos* to Greece. Left 7.3.86.							
Sarepta II	trials pontoon	1947	–	–	11.3.83	–	59, 60
For full story, see text.							
Fordham	inshore minesweeper	1956	–	120	11.7.83	–	52, 68, 117
Hulked, then Bu mid-1990s.							
425	dumb lighter	–	–	–	15.7.83	1,084	117
Sea Merrimac	tug	1964	163	–	18.10.83	30,171	–
Sold with *Sea Volunteer* to Atlantic Tugs for £73,218, 11.83.							
Sea Volunteer	tug	1963	163	–	18.10.83	30,171	–
Ex-Fearless craft	assault craft	–	–	–	28.10.83	11,598	–
Thorngarth	tug	1959	300	–	28.11.83	44,000	117
Resold 1991 as *Carew Castle* then *Falmouth Bay*. Bu La Coruña, Spain, 2011.							
Aragonite	coaster	1958	651	–	5.12.83	36,000	–
Resold Atlantic Towing for £41,485, 12.83.							
RSL 1651	range safety launch	1956	–	12	4.84	–	–
Resold c. 1989 as *Breydon Harrier* then *Gemini Sunset*.							
RSL 1659	range safety launch	1956	–	12	28.6.84	–	–
Resold 1985 as *Kubia*.							
N.S.T 6556(?)	naval stores tender	1966	–	9.5	28.6.84	–	–
Dionissios	cargo vessel	1965	1,165	–	7.84	–	–
Resold G. Harvey, Sittingbourne, as *Nanell*. Left 31.12.84.							
Freshwater	Isle of Wight ferry	1959	363	–	8.84	–	61
Resold 7.86 to Western Ferries (Clyde) as *Sound of Seil*. Bu Garston, 2003.							
Isle of Ely	freighter (BR)	1958	1,492	–	1984	–	–
Resold Bakkers Bruges for Bu, which was complete by 12.85.							
Lough Mahon II	bucket dredger	1964	250	–	1984	–	–
Bought from Cork, resold 8.86.							
Fishbourne	Isle of Wight ferry	1961	1,293	–	1984	–	–
Resold Cyprus as *Kibris 1*. Wrecked 1985.							
Russell	frigate	1957	1,180	6.85	28,880	–	32, 33, 36 37, 49
Bu in East Yard 1985/6. Carefully brought under M275 from West Yard at low tide.							
Telemachus	pontoon		–	–	1.7.85	–	–
Waterwitch	inshore minesweeper/ survey ship	1960	–	120	30.10.85	–	117
Ex-*Powderham*. Sold on by Pounds. Seen at Goole in 1990s as *Old Peculiar*, preservation attempts failed, and she was Bu on Tyne 2006 after sinking at her moorings.							
Gower	tug	1961	152	–	1985	–	–
Resold Greek interests as *Kostas*.							
Yvonne C	diving tender	1946	21	–	1985	–	–
Former *HL(D) 43976*, resold and now houseboat *Enya* at Shoreham-by-Sea.							
Wasperton	coastal minesweeper	1957		360	1985	8,444	–
Former coastal minesweeper, converted to Hong Kong patrol boat. Bu locally in Hong Kong.							
St Margarets	cable vessel	1944	1,959	–	7.2.86	43,388	74, 75, 77
Resold. See pp. 74–5.							
Thatcham	inshore minesweeper	1958	–	120	11.2.86	–	67
Resold to become Greek ferry *Petrakis I* at Corfu.							
42 (S)	lighter	–	–	–	28.11.86	1,084	–
Shipham	inshore minesweeper	1956	–	120	1986	–	68, 117
Bu late 1990s, stern damage maybe preventing resale.							
MFV 119	Admiralty MFV	1944	50	–	1986	–	74, 76, 77
Sandringham	inshore minesweeper	1957	–	170	1986	–	67
Resold and became Greek ferry *Sotirakis I* at Corfu.							
Yarnton	patrol boat	1957		360	1985	8,444	–
Former minesweeper, converted to Hong Kong patrol vessel. Bu locally in Hong Kong.							
Diane K	Sand dredger	1954	398	–	1986	–	–
Former *Auriga*. Resold Greek interests 8.1986.							

Name	Type	Built	GRT	Displnt	Bought	Cost (£)	Text ref
Aveley	inshore minesweeper	1954	–	123	11.86	8,588	–
Ex-Woolwich Sea Cadet vessel 1983–6, in poor condition on arrival. Bu complete by 5.88.							
Brading	ferry	1948	988	–	3.87	–	59, 61, 62
Isle of Wight ferry. Controlled fire at Tipner during Bu, 1994.							
Spurn LV No 14	lightship	1959	300	–	4.87	–	–
Resold Roger Smith, Guernsey. Now at Gloucester as *Sula*, bed and breakfast.							
Protector	patrol vessel	1975	871	–	4.87	68,888	–
Ex-*Seaforth Saga*. Resold as *Marine Protector*, left 4.6.88.							
Guardian	offshore patrol vessel	1975	802	–	5.87	62,688	–
Ex-*Seaforth Champion*. Resold 7.1988 as diamond mining vessel.							
MFV 1048	Admiralty MFV	1943	–	255	1987	–	–
Bu Pounds.							
Glasserton	coastal minesweeper	1958	–	360	12.87	35,308	–
Resold Andover Shipping for Bu Spain. Left 1.1988.							
Whimbrel	trials vessel	1944	300	–	11.12.87	–	52, 75
Bt back by Pounds. Left 22.2.90 with *St Margarets* under tow for Bu Italy but sank on the way.							
Typhoon	naval tug	1960	800	–	1987	–	–
Resold to Greece as *P Typhoon*.							
Sam G	coaster	1962	1,426	–	1988	–	–
Ex-*Helene Russ*. Resold Bilbao for Bu 1989.							
Hazelgarth	tug	1959	230	–	1988	–	–
Resold summer 1988 to Western Ocean Towage Torpoint as *Master Cornishman*.							
Vigilant	customs vessel	1965	–	–	1979	–	117
Resold 1994 for further service. Currently lying at Newhaven.							
Pintail	mooring vessel	1964	766	–	6.1989	37,288	73, 85, 117
Resold Bakkers, Bruges, for Bu 1994.							
MAC 1003	machinery attendant craft	1938	100	–	6.89	–	–
Glenshira	coaster	1953	153	–	1989	–	–
Resold for commercial use and Bu Holyhead, 2004.							
Y8216	patrol boat	–	–	–	1989	–	–
This and the two Y boats below boats Bt from Dutch Navy, Lu ashore. Ultimate fate unknown.							
Y8217	patrol boat	–	–	–	1989	–	–
Y8220	patrol boat	–	–	–	1989	–	–
John W Mackay	cable layer	1922	4,064	–	1990	–	76, 78
Resold Aliaga, Turkey, for scrap. Left under tow, 19.2.1994. Previously Lu Greenwich, 1977–90, where used as backdrop in Indiana Jones film *The Last Crusade*.							
Afan	suction dredger	1961	918	–	1993	–	62
Resold for Bu Bakkers, Bruges, arrived 3.7.93.							
RMAS 1007(S)	stores lighter	1964	150	–	1990	3,388	–
YC 484	mooring lighter	1960	225	–	28.9.90	–	76, 79
Last dockyard lighter employing steam power. To Belgium for preservation but Bu c. 1994.							
NA 249	armament carrier	1944	325	–	3.91	–	–
Became a houseboat at Cowes and then Shoreham.							
NA 332	armament lighter	1956	100	–	1.7.91	–	–
Became a houseboat at Cobden Bridge.							
Otus	submarine	1963	–	1,610	9.8.91	63,388	87, 88, 89, 90
Resold Sassnitz, Germany, as museum exhibit, left 3.6.2002.							
Lightship No 1	light vessel	1946	267	–	7.91	–	80
Resold and became *Mary Mouse II* at Haslar Marina, c. 1994.							
Lightship No 3	light vessel	1947	267	–	27.7.91	20,000	80
Sold 1995 and became radio station *King David* off Israeli coast. Wrecked 2000.							
Lightship No 11	light vessel	1952	267	–	25.7.91	–	80
Resold Rotterdam 5.01 and now a British gastropub in the centre of Rotterdam known as Vessel, 11, or, VII.							
Mandarin	mooring and salvage vessel	1964	766	–	3.92	24,838	–
Resold for commercial use and then Bu Lowestoft, 1995.							
Manly	fleet tender	1982	127	–	1.4.92	37,000	117
Resold for commercial use Brighton 1983 then Almeria, Spain. Bu 2006.							
Mentor	fleet tender	1982	127	–	1992	37,000	–
Resold for commercial use at Falmouth, 3.94.							
Milbrook	fleet tender	1982	127	–	1992	37,000	–
Resold for commercial use at Lymington and then Gloucester.							
Otter	submarine	1962	–	1,603	1992	53,388	87, 117
Bu by Pounds.							

Name	Type	Built	GRT	Displnt	Bought	Cost (£)	Text ref
Opossum	submarine	1964	–	1,603	3.92	–	87
Bu by Pounds.							
ST 1982	US tug	1954	54	–	3.92	–	117
Resold 1995 as yacht *Elektra*.							
ST 2113	US tug	1953	54	–	3.92	–	117
Resold to Read Heavy Lift Towing Florida as *Able Three*.							
ST 1981	US tug	1954	–	–	3.92	–	117
Resold to Read Heavy Lift Towing Florida as *Able Two*.							
Datchet	fleet diving vessel	1972	–	–	1993	42,883	–
Resold for commercial use at Southampton then Gloucester.							
NA 333A	armament carrier	1958	100	–	8.1994	6,188	–
Resold for commercial use as part of fish farm.							
NA 342A	armament carrier	1958	100	–	8.1994	–	–
ST 2115	US tug	1953	54	–	26.1.94	–	–
Resold for further service as *Able One*.							
Orpheus	submarine	1960	–	1,610	9.94	68,888	87, 89, 90
Bu by Pounds.							
Oracle	submarine	1963	–	1,610	9.1994	–	56, 87, 88, 89, 90
Resold Aliaga, Turkey, for Bu but sank under tow. See Appendix 3.							
Opportune	submarine	1964	–	1,610	1994	–	87, 88
Bu by Pounds.							
Kinbrace	mooring and salvage vessel	1945	775	–	1994	–	–
Resold 9.1994.							
BS 6099	military lighter	–	–	–	1994	–	–
BC 6098	military lighter	–	–	–	1994	–	–
Resold Dordrecht.							
BC 6547	military lighter	–	–	–	1994	–	–
Resold Dordrecht							
BC 6459	military lighter	–	–	–	1994	–	–
One of several ex-US Army lighters on Portchester moorings.							
NA 342	armament lighter	–	–	–	1994	–	–
Resold for commercial use as fish farm.							
Boltby	stern trawler	1974	325	–	26.10.94	–	–
Ex-*Boltby Queen*. Resold by 1997 for commercial use in Spain.							
Magpie	target	1961	330	–	1.1995	3,321	–
Former trawler *Hondo*. Resold for service in Spain as trawler.							
Nordic	barge	–	–	–	4.95	–	–
Pochard	MSV	1973	923		6.95	34,888	–
Bu 1996 at Tipner.							
Nurton	coastal minesweeper	1957	–	360	6.95	48,388	66
Resold Dawn Premier Services for Bu at Selby, Yorkshire.							
RMAS 1415(U)	sullage lighter	1964	100	–	9.8.95	2,138	–
Targe	target	1962	273	–	9.8.95	3,321	–
Former trawler *Erimo*.							
Waterspout	water tank vessel	1967	285	–	1995	34,788	–
Resold for commercial use in Gibraltar.							
Golden Cross	tug	1955	132	–	1995	–	–
Resold for commercial use. Bu 2014, Rosneath.							
Waterfowl	water tank vessel	1974	285	–	30.1.96	3,626	–
Resold for commercial use in Trinidad.							
NA 327 (A)	armament carrier	1956	100	–	29.3.96	1,813	–
NA 250 (A)	armament carrier	1943	325	–		1,813	–
City of Bristol	dredger	1969	1,092	–	14.8.96	–	–
Resold for commercial use, 1.99.							
City of Southampton	dredger	1969	996	–	14.8.96	–	–
Resold for commercial use, 9.97.							
YC476	sullage lighter	1958	83	–	1996	2,188	–
Alston	effluent tanker	1968	836	–	1996	–	–
Former *Leadsman*. Resold for commercial service in Greece, 4.1997.							
YD 206	US crane pontoon	–	–	–	1996	–	–
Towed on purchase from Rota, near Cadiz.							
RMAS 1014(S)	stores lighter	1966	82	–	1996	3,277	–

Name	Type	Built	GRT	Displnt	Bought	Cost (£)	Text ref
RMAS 1015(U)	sullage lighter	1966	82	–	22.4.97	4,137	–
Resold as fuel pontoon at Itchen Marine Towage, American Wharf.							
RMAS 1017(S)	stores lighter	1968	82	–	22.4.97	4,477	–
RMAS 1101(S)	stores lighter	1964	115	–	22.4.97	6,337	–
Resold for commercial use at Itchen Marine as no 10.							
RMAS 1006(S)	stores lighter	1964	150	–	22.4.97	3,177	–
MAC 1009	machinery attendant craft	1968	182	–	22.4.97	16,787	–
Resold after generator removed.							
MAC 1002	machinery attendant craft	1942	178	–	22.4.97	–	–
Bu 1.97 as unsound structure.							
Sheraton	coastal minesweeper	1956	–	360	12.97	51,877	64, 65, 66
Bu Tipner to 2002.							
Brinton	coastal minesweeper	1954	–	360	12.97	51,377	64, 109
Bu Tipner from 2002.							
Loyal Watcher	diving tender	1978	112	–	12.97	67,377	–
Resold to Deep Blue Diving.							
Oilbird	oil carrier	1969	352	–	12.97	–	–
Resold as *Rockfish* to Blands of Gibraltar, 11.1999.							
Dittisham	inshore minesweeper	1954	–	120	1997	–	66
Bu 1997 after engine removed.							
S.H.B. Seahorse	buoy laying vessel	1958	156	–	1.98	–	–
Had 'horns' removed in East Yard, then reported to be sold for further service.							
Oilwell	oil carrier	1969	280	–	1.7.98	–	–
Resold as *Dragonfish* to Blands of Gibraltar.							
Oilman	oil carrier	1969	280	–	22.7.98	–	–
Resold for commercial use in Ireland as *Pater*.							
Bullseye	Target towing ship	1962	273	–	29.10.98	–	88
Former trawler *Tokio*, Bt by Admiralty to tow targets and then bt by Pounds. Resold for use as houseboat, Bu 2007.							
Brave Swordsman	MTB	1958	–	114	1998	–	–
Had been used as target by RN, Bt by Hayden Baillie Collection, Southampton, stripped for spares for *Brave Challenger*, then Bu.							
PA30-31	LCVP Mk II	1966	8.5	–	c. 1998	–	94, 97
Restored and now on display at Le Grand Bunker Museum, Ouistreham, France.							
PA30-10	LCVP Mk II	1965	8.5	–	c. 1998	–	94, 97
Now displayed on a roundabout at Shoreham-by-Sea, Sussex.							
Salveda	salvage vessel	–	–	–	c. 1998	–	–
Kaptaube	coaster	1930?	147	–	1998	–	–
Former *Meta Grete, Wilfried*.							
Poseidon	customs seizure	–	–	–	15.12.98	–	–
Avenir	coaster	1962	390	–	–	–	–
Another customs seizure. Bu Tipner *c*. 2002.							
Kingston	tug	1962	113	–	1999?	–	–
Former *Sun XXIII*.							
Thor	crane barge	–	–	–	1999	–	–
Towed from Queenborough.							
Astrapi	fast patrol vessel	1962	–	–	–	–	–
Muirhead	barge	–	–	–	1997?	–	–
Bibury	fleet tender	1964	77	–	14.12.99	–	–
Became a houseboat at Hoo St Werburgh on the Medway in Kent.							
Deep Diver	buoy tender	–	–	–	c. 2000	–	–
Bu 2002.							
Caisson	caisson	–	–	–	2000	–	56
LARC LX50	landing craft	–	–	–	–	–	–
One of two in East Yard, the other owned by A.F. Ross and Sons of Girvan. Bu.							
Wilton	coastal minesweeper	1973	–	450	8.2001	–	–
First glass reinforced plastic (GRP) warship in the world. Resold to Essex Yacht Club, Leigh-on-Sea, 8.2001, for use as their clubhouse.							
Stalker	ex-Submarine Support and LST (3)	1947	–	2,256	10.2002	–	74, 95, 98, 109
Bu finished by 2012.							
Vigilant	customs vessel	1902	124	–	1992	–	79
Left 2007 for restoration at Faversham. Now probably Lu at Gillingham, Kent, with Medway Maritime Trust.							

Name	Type	Built	GRT	Displnt	Bought	Cost (£)	Text ref
Betty	tug	1963	40	–	2004	–	–
Bu Pounds, 11.04.							
504(F)	unknown	–	–	–	2004	–	–
Fulford	coastal tanker	1960	477	–	2004	–	–
Greendale H	effluent vessel	1962	311	–	2004	–	–
Bu at Pounds, lifted onshore for Bu by *Apache* crane.							
Carmel	coaster	1971	199	–	2005	–	–
Sold 8.20 but still Lu on Pounds' moorings in 2025.							
Oliver Felix	tug	1962	144	–	2008	–	–
Former *Lovely Jubbly, Polgarth*. Bu 2011.							
Douglas McWilliam	waste disposal vessel	1983	172	–	2009	–	–
Bu on arrival Tipner.							
Abbira	tug	1965	–	–	2010	–	–
Bu Tipner, 2010/11. Arrested River Itchen 2008, as drug runner.							
Joan	tug	1974	89	–	20.10.10	–	*111, 113*
Arrived Tipner, 2013, previously Lu River Itchen. Bu 3.21.							
RNAL 50	flying platform	1957	237	–	4.11	–	*53*
Ex-*RN AIR 50*. Bu Tipner April/May 2013.							
Nancy	tug	1974	89	–	c. 2013	–	*111, 113*
Arrived Tipner, 2013, previously Lu River Itchen, Bu 12.20.							
Chief/The Chief	tug	1930	72	–	2013	–	–
Bu 12.2012.							
TI	landing craft	2010	–	–	2013	–	–
Resold Canada 2015.							
Apache	floating crane	1952	1,246	–	2015	–	*49, 109, 111*
ex-US Army *Pine Ridge BD - 6073*. Assisted in bu of several ships by lifting them onshore. Bu itself 4.21–3.22.							
Canute	floating crane	1969	232	–	9.14	–	*109, 111, 113*
Ex-Southampton Harbour Board (SHB), Bt Wilton Netherlands as Mammoet, crane section, Bu 2023. Pontoon hull still at Tipner as we go to press.							
Hamnfjord	trawler	1905	140	–	11.16	–	*111, 112*
Bu 2.2022. Last ship to be Bu at Pounds.							
Uriah Heep	ferry	1999	–	–	–	–	–
Ex-Hythe–Southampton ferry, resold to Jetstream Tours on the Thames, 2018.							
Onyx Mariner	tank barge	–	188	–	–	–	–
Resold as houseboat on the Medway, 10.2018.							
Hen	barge	1925	115	–	12.2	–	*112*
Converted to houseboat and left for Bembridge, 2022.							
King Harry Chain Ferry no VI	floating bridge	1974	–	–	2010	–	–
Superstructure removed 2010–12. Probably Bu in 2023 yard clearance.							
Idun Viking	hovercraft	1997	–	–	–	–	*73*
Pounds acquired cockpit (only) of this hovercraft and resold to private buyer.							
Susan	tug	1973	80	–	11.17	–	*111*
Previously Lu Hythe, Bu 3–6.2018. (ex-RMAS *Felicity*).							
Vortex Agwi	workboat	–	–	–	7.19	–	–
Resold 2023 to Marine Farm Services for service in Devon.							

NB: 1976 cost figures in italics are all expressed in US$, not £.

APPENDIX 3

HMS *ORACLE*: A MURKY END IN 2004

The fate of *Oracle* is recalled here in a 2004 report:

> *For years she was an unloved landmark rusting in a scrapyard besides the busy motorway linking Portsmouth with the outside world. A relic of the Cold War naval top brass had long since decided they no longer had any use for Her Majesty's Submarine Oracle. Despite half-hearted attempts to save her the Oberon class boat was always doomed – although few could have predicted the manner of her demise. There were cheers and tears when the 2,000-ton hulk left Pounds yard at Tipner on 30 October 2004 towed by a powerful German tug. The sea going Fairplay XIV had been hired to deliver the sub to Turkish breakers. Seven days later the tug was spotted on radar heading eastward through the Straits of Gibraltar. But she seemed to be fast to have a vessel in tow, according to puzzled onlookers. Then she was seen to put into Ceuta in Morocco where she stayed for three days before setting off for the Portuguese capital Lisbon. On November 18, the tug was again off Ceuta, leaving enthusiasts wondering what on earth had happened to the submarine. Full details are sketchy, but it soon became clear that the old sub was now lying on the seabed somewhere off Gibraltar. The towline had been cut after she sprang a catastrophic leak. Experts reckon Fairplay XIV was travelling at seven to eight knots with the sub in tow, when it should have been doing no more than five knots. The vessel was also heading into Force Seven conditions, when a prudent skipper would have abandoned the trip in anything more than Force Five. Harry Pounds who owns the Tipner yard and sold Oracle to the Turks is still unsure precisely what happened – but he has his suspicions. 'According to everyone I've spoken to the tug was towing too fast in a force seven', he says. The 44-year-old submarine couldn't take the strain and went down. Harry compares it to a juggernaut towing a mini. 'If the car starts to wobble, the truck driver probably won't notice until it's too late and the car rolls over.' He reckons Fairplay's skipper found himself in a similar predicament.*
>
> *'It was a huge tug, much too big for the job. It had a bollard pull of about fifty tons when normally twenty are ample for a sub. They went through the storm, going a bit faster than they should have done. Water got in and flooded the decks. The tug had a problem, but the tow was a quarter of a mile behind. I think he realised in the morning he was in trouble, but it was too late… Britain's Marine Accident Investigation Branch aren't interested as the sub was no longer UK registered and she went down in international waters.'*
>
> *It's not known how much the Turkish yard paid for Oracle although the Russians have sold similar sized Foxtrot subs for £20,000 and the Turks have been known to pay double the going rate in the UK for scrap metal. 'It wasn't a fortune, but it wasn't peanuts either,' said Harry. The Turkish scrap metal dealer is now trying to sue the Hamburg based Fairplay Towage for the loss. But the Germans say they're not to blame […] Joerg Mainzer, the firm's managing director says 'The submarine was in a really weak state. Bushes were growing out of her bow. She'd been lying in Portsmouth for ages and didn't make a very good impression […] the weather conditions were quite normal. There was some wind earlier on.' But it's not the first time Fairplay XIV has failed to deliver. In March 2003, the 5200 horsepower tug was hired to tow a redundant cruise liner, the Ryndam, from Alabama in the USA to breakers in India. The 50-year-old ship never reached her destination sinking at a depth of 2,500 metres off the Dominican Republic. Joerg says, 'It happens now and again. It was bad luck.'*[61]

Note from author: *Oracle* had arrived at Pounds in 1994 (see more detail on pp. 87–90), so had been moored there for ten years. However, the purchaser would presumably have undertaken a survey prior to her being towed away.

Another shipbreaker describes the difficulties of towing a submarine for scrap:

The way you tow a set of submarines is with a large tug, a long wire from her to the first sub, then a long wire from that to the second, and so on – all strung out in a straight line. The wires are really long, ½ a mile or so. Towing a dead ship, which has no way to pump water out of itself if it gets a leak, is a risk for the tug, which needs to have time to release the cable should the dead ship start to go under. You go for a lengthy cable, so that if there's a problem you've got long enough. That's true for any ship, but for a sub, which is mainly below water even when she's on the surface, it's a lot truer – so longer cable. One of the risk areas for a submarine that is being towed for scrap is where the prop shaft enters the hull. [...] Generally, the hull of a sub is impressively leak-proof, but anywhere that an item penetrates it is vulnerable, and particularly so if, for example, there has been work done to remove the prop as that may have loosened the seals around the shaft.[62]

Paid cheques from 1950. *(Pounds)*

Endnotes

1 Trade directories and rate books reviewed in Portsmouth Central Library.

2 Ibid.

3 The excellent local history website www.luppitt.net has material about the Devon village where Elizabeth Pounds (née Baker) was born in 1830.

4 A search in June 2021 by Portsmouth Royal Dockyard Historical Trust of pay/employment records 1860/1900 confirmed Frederick Pounds did not work in the Dockyard.

5 To this day, press reports occasionally incorrectly refer to the 'John Pounds' scrapyard. In 1999 his reputation was confirmed when readers of a local newspaper awarded him 'Man of the Millennium', beating Nelson and other more obvious candidates.

6 Peter N. Lockyer, 'Wooden Ships in Hampshire – Launching, Breaking and Disposal, 1700–1850', unpublished thesis.

7 Trade directories, Portsmouth Central Library.

8 TNA AIR76/ 410, AIR79/2753, WO339/131756.

9 See V44V 82_SiteReport1_February2016.pdf (maritimearchaeologytrust.org).

10 23 March 1964 £7,500 to HG Pounds, 13 April 1964 £6,500, 8 June 1964 £4,000.

11 Land Registry search of title number HP108656 dated 22 May 2020.

12 Portchester Castle had facilities to hold at least 7,500 French and Dutch prisoners, 1794–1814.

13 TNA BT 297/736 Hall, Pain, and Foster letter of 25 March 1926, solicitors acting for owners of plots.

14 Copy letter, reproduced from TNA BT 297/736.

15 Portsmouth Council letter of 24 January 1939.

16 Ibid.

17 Files in Pounds family collection.

18 TNA BT 356/3712, HG Pounds letter of November 1936.

19 TNA BT 356/3712, Manuscript note by unknown person at bottom of note dated 12 August 1937 by a Mr Wright of Board of Trade noting no progress on break-up of 'derelicts'.

20 Land Registry Search 22 May 2020 on title number HP108656.

21 *The News*, April 1965.

22 TNA BT 356/3712 Letter of Alldhuis to Board of Trade, 9 August 1947.

23 Shipbuilding and Shipping Record, 6 August 1946.

24 Dr Ian Buxton, 'The Tank Landing Craft Mark 4', *Warships*, nos 198–200, WSS, 2020.

25 Land Registry search of title HP108656 dated 22 May 2020.

26 R. Holme, *Cairnryan Military Port 1940–1996: From U-Boats to the Ark Royal* (Wigtown: GC Books, 1997).

27 TNA WO 32/19170 Letter to J. Brewis MP, 7 October 1960.

28 TNA WO 32/19170 Note by Hugh Fraser to Pannell MP, 3 December 1959.

29 TNA WO 32/19170 Loose minute, 23 November 1959.

30 TNA WO 32/19170.

31 TNA WO 32/19170 Letter Command Land Agent to War Office, 25 March 1960.

32 TNA WO 32/19170 Ministry of Transport, etc., 13 October 1960.

33 Hansard 1 March 1961.

34 Estimate by Ian Watson, former managing director of Shipbreaking (Queenborough) Ltd and associated company Queenborough Rolling Mill, once Europe's leading reprocessor of railway track. Much of the track, sleepers, panels and associated equipment would have been reused and thus would attract a much higher sale value than if for scrap.

35 TNA WO 32/19170 Note from John Profumo to Rt Hon M. Redmayne MO.

36 Through Pounds company, Paulsgrove Salvage and Trading Company.

37 See photograph on p. 29.
38 TNA Letter from City of Portsmouth Estates Department 18 February 1963 to War Office.
39 TNA DEFE 31/8 Auction report 2 November 1964
40 TNA DEFE 31/8 Memo by V.G. Hibberd dated 2 November 1964.
41 Dates of construction and details from www.britishlistedbuildings.co.uk.
42 Incorporated on 14 January 1965. Company 00834220. The company is referred to as owner of West Yard in City of Portsmouth Planning Committee minutes, *c*. 1973.
43 *The News*, 27 January 2005.
44 *The News*, 25 November 1997. Pounds comments by Tony Pounds-Cornish.
45 Ibid.
46 *The News*, 14 June 1978.
47 Perhaps as many as 3,000 were broken up, according to discussions with Tony Pounds-Cornish.
48 The British Iron and Steel Corporation (BISCO) was effectively owned by the British steel industry and until 1962 allocated ships to specific UK shipbreakers for demolition.
49 SI papers at Marine Technology Special Collection, Newcastle University.
50 An excellent article on *C1* can be found on the website of the Gosport History Club: David Maber, 'Growing Up with the Hulk', https://gosporthistoryclub.org.uk/gosport-history-archive-index/growing-up-with-the-hulk.
51 Courtesy of *The News*, 17 February 1989.
52 *The News* October 2000.
53 See www.hms-otus.com.
54 *The News*, 30 August 1997.
55 *After the Battle* magazine, no. 103, 'Spielberg's Day' (1999), describes this in detail.
56 The film can be found on YouTube at https://youtu.be/LfwRc2bdzXg. It is well worth looking at.
57 War Office subsumed by Ministry of Defence in 1964.
58 See https://youtu.be/LfwRc2bdzXg.
59 Winston Ramsey, 'Portsmouth Graveyard', *After the Battle*, no. 37 (1982).
60 *The News*, February 1993.
61 Courtesy of *The News*, 29 November, 2004.
62 Comment by Ian Watson, former MD of Shipbreaking (Queenborough) Ltd. In 1990, they lost an ex-Russian submarine being towed to their yard at Cairnryan.

BIBLIOGRAPHY AND SOURCES

A. Primary Sources for the Ship List in Appendix 2

This list could not have been compiled without the help of the Pounds family, who have most generously lent the author accounting records for the businesses particularly for the period of the 1960s to the 1980s, as well as some bills of sale, paid cheques and correspondence files. They have also provided schedules of some ships acquired.

- Numerous maritime historians, listed in the Acknowledgements on p. 144, have provided invaluable assistance.
- Dr Ian Buxton and the late Brian Hargreaves kindly referred me to two manuscript ledgers of the Contracts and Purchases Branch detailing Royal Navy disposals 1916 to 1939 in the Admiralty Library at Portsmouth. They are referenced CP.8A and were very helpful in identifying early Pounds acquisitions and prices paid. Sadly, no similar references exist for post-1939 disposals, although details of bids made by breakers, including Pounds, for six submarines in 1971/2 were found at the RN Submarine Museum, with the kind help of George Malcolmson. On HMS *Trump*, for example, Pounds' offer of £31,280 was narrowly beaten by a bid of £33,400 by Cashmores of Newport.
- Dave Sowdon was also very helpful and recounts his sources in identifying 181 craft sold to Pounds from 1976 to 1988 by the Directorate of Marine Services (Naval). Also to previous disposals (1958–76) by the Port Auxiliary Service (PAS) and prior to that (1926–58), to the Admiralty Yard Craft Service. He recalled:

I was able to borrow all their record cards for powered and dumb vessels, and I transcribed them all. I also repaired and re-stapled their record cards so they went back to Bath in a better condition than they left. I understand that the record cards are now in the Naval Historical Branch in Portsmouth and nigh-on inaccessible these days. Therefore, the source is official. Vessels were sold, over time, by various agencies on behalf of the Yardcraft Service, PAS and later RMAS.

These vessels were typically tugs, tenders, lighters, salvage vessels and other small yard craft, prefixed with the letters A, Y or RMAS when not specifically named.

- Freedom of Information Request – 'MOD Minute detailing RN ships disposed of 1980/98, dates and sale prices', 1999. This detailed, inter alia, Pounds' acquisitions of forty-two ships and prices paid 1980–98. Obtained by Brian Hargreaves.
- Lloyds Registers and Lloyds Casualty Returns. Also, Lloyds Register 'Confidentials' were reviewed for 1960 to 1991. This biennial publication lists merchant ships over 300 tons owned by various shipowners, including Pounds. The year of arrival is shown, often as well as their ultimate fate.
- With the kind permission of the Pounds family, the author has made visits to the Tipner yard on several occasions since 1991. 27 September 1991, 14 February 1994, 13 March 1995, 1 February 1997, 21 August 1998, 23 July 1999, 18 November 1999, 13 November 2000, 11 May 2001, 8 July 2011, 8 December 2017, 11 January 2018, 6 February 2018, 8 November 2022. Two visits were also made to Fort Southwick.

B. Other Primary Sources

Files at the National Archives Kew (TNA)
Royal Flying Corps record – H.G. Pounds 1914/21 WO 339/131758
Portchester 1925/47 BT 297/ 736
'Sales of obsolete RN vessels 1925/33' MT /9/2187
Buying Hopper 8 1933 RAIL 252/2243
Portchester 1938 BT 356/3712
Tipner 1953 BT 356/3384
Tipner 1954 BT 356/7070
Tipner sale 1958/65 DEFE 51/8
Tipner jetty 1964 BT 356/3457
Tipner jetty 1964 BT 356/5974
Cairnryan sale to Pounds WO 32/19170

Marine Technology Special Collection, Newcastle University
Dr Ian Buxton kindly referred me to files on bids by other shipbreakers to ships acquired by Pounds.

C. Secondary Sources
For the early days, the excellent local history site www.luppitt.net has material about the Devon village of Luppitt, where Elizabeth Pounds (née Baker) was baptised in 1830. The current Pounds family regard Elizabeth as the founder of their core marine business which lasted until 2023.

Buxton, Dr Ian, 'The Tank Landing Craft Mark 4', *Warships*, nos 198–200, WSS, 2020.
Cowsill, Miles, *By Road across the Sea* (Ramsey: Ferry Publications, 1990).
Holme, Richard, *Cairnryan Military Port 1940–1996: From U-Boats to the Ark Royal* (Wigtown: GC Books, 1997).

The excellent *After the Battle* magazine (afterthebattle.com) covered Pounds on two occasions:
- Issue no. 37, 'Portsmouth Graveyard' (1982) – report on a visit in 1978 by the then editor Winston Ramsey to view tanks and military vehicles. Extract and photos are reproduced in Chapter 5, pp. 103–106.
- Issue no. 103, 'Spielberg's Day' (1999) – making of the *Saving Private Ryan* film, as covered in Chapter 5, pp. 94–8.

The excellent Facebook page 'Portsmouth Shipbreaking – Pounds Scrapyard', run by Pounds expert Stephen Wenham.

For naval ships, the following reference works were invaluable:
Colledge, J.J., *Ships of the Royal Navy* (London: Seaforth Publishing, 2022).
Janes Fighting Ships (London: Janes, multiple years). A well-known annual publication.

For merchant ships, the following annual publications (published by Lloyds Register of Shipping (London) were very useful:
- *Lloyds Register*
- *Lloyds Casualty Returns*

ACKNOWLEDGEMENTS

Acknowledgements and thanks are due to:

Harry Pounds, John Henry Pounds, Tony Pounds-Cornish* and his wife Gay. Also, *The News* Portsmouth, National Museum of the Royal Navy, Navy News, RN Submarine Museum Gosport, Portsmouth Local Studies Library, Portsmouth City Museum and Records Service, the University of Portsmouth as well as Linda Allen, Roger Allen*, David Asprey, Paul Baker, Richard Barnes, David Baynes, Dr Paul Brown, Dr Ian Buxton, Dr Ann Coats, Kim Corner, Peter Dawson*, Sid Dean*, Anna Delaney, Cliff Dredge*, T.W. Ferrers Walker*, John Freestone*, 'Biff' Fricker*, David Fricker, Charlotte Frost, Robin Hinson, Rona Holme, Tom Holme, Ian Gregg, Lisa Hands, Brian Hargreaves*, Dave Hill, Andrew Humphreys*, Freddie Huxtable, Mike Jackson, Tom Lee, Peter Lockyer, George Malcolmson, Andrew Mason, Dennis Maxted*, Gil Mayes, Dr Brian Newman*, Jill Penny, Winston Ramsey, Sara Ratcliffe, Barry Robertson, Philip Simons, Dave Sowdon, Deryk Swetnam, Steven Tacey, Gavin Theobald-Moulds, Ian Watson, Stephen Wenham, Frank Wood.

Apologies to those I have omitted. Sadly, those marked * have now 'crossed the bar'.

I thank ACJM, MDG, SRC, RABC, RFJ, NDC and of course D, for their encouragement throughout.

Finally, many thanks to Rob Gardiner, Julian Mannering and all at Seaforth for their encouragement and for organising publication of the book.

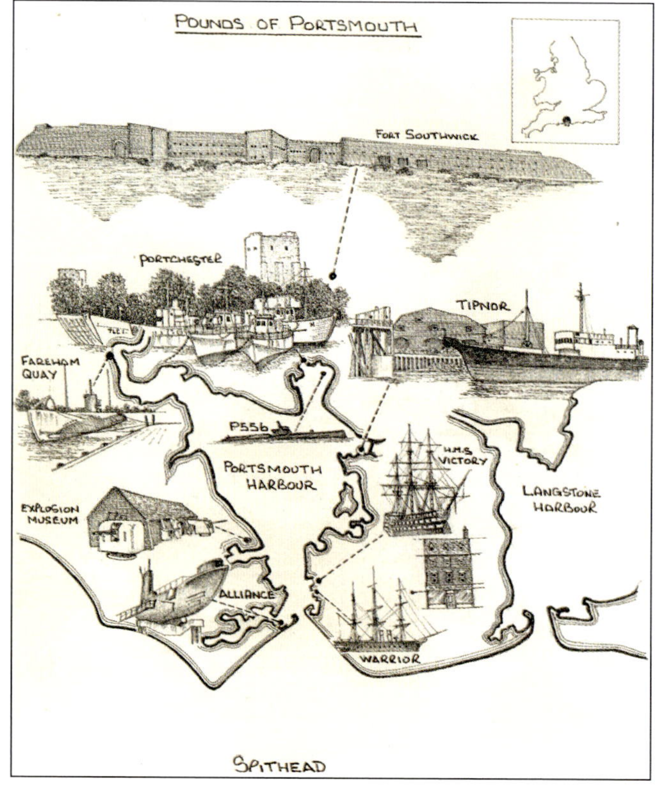

A map showing the Pounds sites at Fareham (1921), Portchester (1924–67), Tipner (1953–2023) and Fort Southwick (2003–). *(Barry Robertson)*